Robert Adair

A Whig's Apology for his Consistency

In a Letter from a Member of Parliament to his Friend in the borough of ****

Robert Adair

A Whig's Apology for his Consistency
*In a Letter from a Member of Parliament to his Friend in the borough of * * * ***

ISBN/EAN: 9783337106935

Printed in Europe, USA, Canada, Australia, Japan

Cover: Foto ©ninafisch / pixelio.de

More available books at **www.hansebooks.com**

A

WHIG's APOLOGY

FOR

HIS CONSISTENCY;

IN

A LETTER

FROM

A MEMBER OF PARLIAMENT

TO

[HIS FRIEND

IN THE BOROUGH OF * * * *.

London:

Printed for J, DEBRETT, oppofite Burlington
Houfe, Piccadilly,

1705.

A WHIG's APOLOGY, &c. &c.

SIR,

THE intelligence you send me from **** is by no means unexpected. Popularity has seldom been attached to the sentiments of a Whig. Whether he acts in a party, or individually pursues the dictates of his conscience, the true, consistent Whig never steps aside from his purpose to close in with the prevailing politics of the day. Educated in this way of thinking, I have always, as you know very well, entertained a great dislike for schemes which profess to please all parties. No man succeeds at this game who holds any serious opinions of his duty. Wise, or honest politicians never try it. In the awful period of our affairs which we have now reached, where scarcely a choice is left except between the worst extremes, perhaps it is not easy to please ourselves. Yet more difficult is it so to shape and fashion our opinions, as to produce a common sentiment among any

B

considerable number of persons. But at once to satisfy those who may be disposed to agree, to conciliate those who differ, and to preserve our own consistency, seems a young and sanguine hope with little except its benevolence to recommend it. You must not, therefore, expect from me testimonies of any stronger feeling than regret, on hearing that several of my constituents at ****, yourself among the number, have expressed dissatisfaction in regard to some parts of my late conduct in Parliament. To your sense and candour I am now about to submit an explanation of its motives, and entreat that through your means it may receive the same advantages of circulation and publicity which have not, I find, been denied to the calumnies that were meant to ruin me in your esteem.

You will acknowledge by this proceeding, as I hope you will soon discover by the sentiments it is intended to convey, how little I am disposed to quit that middle path in which, as your representative, and in unison with your wishes, I have journeyed on for so many years. You will see that I have neither the expectation of improving our own state of things by any infusion of the new principles, nor think the mischief with which we are threatened by their prevalence to be averted by the dereliction of those on which I have conceived the whole

of my public pretensions to rest : that I can
neither soften the inveteracy of opinions
imbibed from the earliest times, and confirmed by the observation of every day,
which compel me to look to the system on
which government is administered as the
source of every ill that has befallen us, nor
change the habits by which my conduct has
been regulated to a moderate indeed, but to
a decided course, in compliance with any
modern superstitions, or with the terrors
they inspire.   Strengthened and supported
by these habits, they did in effect determine
my choice in the hour of doubt which first
divided us, and must govern and guide me
through the tempest when doubt and deli-
beration shall be no more.   I know that it
will be far from an easy task to keep our
balance.   Extreme liberty and extreme
law, anarchy and arbitrary power, and all
the evils of both, will alternately be danced
before our eyes, as it may suit the purpose
of eloquence to persuade, or of artifice to
puzzle us.   All that we, plain unrefining
men, have been labouring to settle in our
minds under the impression of a stationary
duty, will be assailed through our fears,
through our hopes, and possibly through
our affections.   We must endeavour to resist them all.   Alike unwilling and unable
to investigate the subtlety of contending
theories, we know that there is one safe,

easy track in which, while we are content to tread, we can never miss our way.
Where imagination is likely to mislead, or
passion to disturb, or sagacity to fail, we
must have recourse to our memories and
experience.

I own to you Sir, that I look upon these
times, big as they seem with events too
mighty for our speculations, with infinitely
less apprehension as far as my own actions
may be concerned in them, from having,
as I must think, begun at the right end, and
impressed my mind very early with a persuasion that the Whig doctrine I was em-
bracing was true, wise, practicable, and
would be serviceable to me in all difficulties: that it was a doctrine from which no
circumstances of convenience could justify
my departure, as it was itself formed very
much upon a principle of convenience, and
even had in it something of foresight into
the perilous extremities with which we are
threatened. I had imagined it to be one
great quality of these principles, in the
doubtful crisis of public ferment when all
things else are fluctuating and insecure, to
keep the mind of him who should profess
them collected and unshaken; nor was it
wholly without a view to such a time that I
confirmed and invigorated myself in them;
in order not to be caught unawares, and in
the midst of confusion and trouble to have

that to seek which chiefly in such a moment I should want to use. To be ever pressing as far as they will go, discussions upon obedience and responsibility; to be even limiting, and distinguishing, and defining where submission should end, and resistance begin; to be habitually putting cases upon the supposed ruin of the constitution, I hold to be a most unwise practice; but perhaps it is as bad to make no provision in our own minds for these disastrous possibilities. Indeed there passes not a day which does not discover to him who has gained it, the full value of such dangerous knowledge.

You will neither find me therefore in what I offer you, making use of " principles too big for my purpose," nor compromising, I hope, in one single thought or expression the fair cause of liberty, in whatever corner of the world she displays her banner. Ill would he deserve to be your representative who proves recreant to that cause. But the liberty I most love, is that by which I have most been benefitted,—a plain, practical liberty, such as she is to be found in the British constitution, where she resides, and through which she acts. Very warmly disposed towards the liberty of other countries, I acknowledge my chief solicitude to be for that of my own. I can support no government therefore, which does not both in its construction and in its march, discover the inclination and the means of providing for, and securing this liberty, not agreeable to vague and capricious fancies, but according to the provisions of known law, the long received interpretations of custom, and the examples of the best men in the best times. Every attempt to administer government in any other manner, every system that either from some error in its plan, or some great depravity in the persons chosen to give it effect, is not capable of being made to harmonize with these principles, I hold to be vicious, destructive, and such as to call for our opposition to it by all lawful methods. If upon the occurrence of any extraordinary emergency, there should arise a necessity of co-operating with those who for the time being are entrusted with the direction of the public force, it will be incumbent upon all Persons who think in general as I do, upon the subject of government, carefully to distinguish a casual support, which necessity rather extorts than preference bestows, from that personal confidence which arises from the opinion that power is in the hands of those who deserve it most, and can use it best. But the duty of general mistrust remains unaltered. It is of a severe, vigilant, active quality ; and any suspension of it demands, *prima facie,* an explanation, which

I will not deny may either be found in the notoriety of imminent danger, or deduced from the reasonable probability of it. I have ever been of the number of those who reject the doctrine of agency, and deny that members of parliament are bound at all times, and indiscriminately, to obey what are called instructions from their constituents. But if you admit (as I think you do) to me that, as members of parliament, we are not in a state of servile dependence which precludes in what we do for your service all exercise of our discretion, we must concede, on our side, that in charging ourselves with so heavy a trust we make ourselves parties to a cause the very first obligation of which is to see it to its end: not to abandon the conclusion of it on any sudden caprice of ours, or in obedience to any foreign impulse whatever. Taking upon us to judge of what is best for those who send us hither, they surely will have just ground of complaint against us if we are led off from the practical duties of the public life we have embraced by whims and fancies, or driven into the arms of what we think in our consciences a corrupt, an incapable, and a treacherous administration, by the dread, forsooth, that our perseverance in hostility to it will afford aid to some silly projectors. They must think us mere triflers indeed if we suffer these ter-

rors not only to disarm our vigilance, but
to invade our dearest attachments, and triumph over formed and solid friendships,
the growth of many years, and many tri-
als. For myself I will frankly acknowledge that I would rather obtain the character of a diligent member of parliament,
constantly and assiduously in his place,
watching the conduct of ministers, than be
the author of any one of those contrivances which is to perfect our crazy system,
and drive away strife and wickedness from
the world, or even the most renowned of
those dissertations in which alone the memory of such projects will live by the eloquence with which they are reprobated.
In these narrow trammels your representative is content to walk, nor is he disgusted with the humility of his pursuits by
the consideration that to execute their objects with fidelity has hitherto been found
sufficient to employ the largest faculties of
the human mind during the longest period
alloted to human existence, is a scope for
the most active benevolence, and the highest virtue, and the proudest genius that
ever illuminated the earth.

If such feelings unfit me for an association either with those lofty spirits who
would regenerate, or those who would en-
slave mankind, they suit at least the sphere
in which it has been your will that I should

move. They have taught me to be content
with the good within my reach, and to
preserve for you and defend to the utmost
that which I have ever esteemed a system of real and substantial liberty. What
shall be our course hereafter, perhaps it is
in the sagacity of few to discern, and in
the power of none to determine. We are,
indeed, in a situation the dangers of which
I can limit to no description, or degree: a
situation in which the ills we know not,
scarcely can suppress the ills we have; one
from which if ever we escape we shall owe
more to chance and patience than I fear
either to our wisdom or our virtue. Ministers themselves have told you that it
can no longer be dissembled. I write to
you Sir, indeed, under the most awful impressions. I conceive myself to be taking
a solemn and a last leave of all that from
my infancy I have held dear in the political
establishment of my country. This contest has generated a way of thinking on
the topics of ordinary life so intirely its
own that whatever may be the end of our
present troubles I see little hope of reviv-
ing any one genuine constitutional feeling
among us. I know not how it may strike
you and the generality of those for whom
this letter is meant, but for myself I have
the sad consolation of reflecting that it
does not come upon me by surprize. For

C

this day of death I have been long preparing. Early and continued adversity has
taught me in what posture to receive the
blow. Take it not amiss therefore, that, in
this temper of mind, I think lightly of the
value of any defence or apology whatever;
or that what I offer should be rather in the
spirit of warning to you, than vindication
of myself. I am far from indifferent to
the good opinion of my fellow-citizens in
general: least of all to your's, to whom
have been dedicated the labours of my life:
but we have now reached that state from
which all factitious relations must disap-
pear. The reward of honest service, or
the punishment of guilty versatility must
wait the decision of an age yet too distant
from our own to be swayed by any common reciprocations of esteem or flattery
between us. He that is thoroughly impressed with a sense of this as of a truth he
is about to experience, feels himself in a situation in which, if he cannot be silent, it is
easiest for him to be sincere. Nothing remains to divert his attention from the scene
that is closing upon his eyes. Nothing on
this side society to interest his hopes or
alarm his fears. His exertions have been
given to his country; his accounts are ready; the rest is for his fame.

Had I therefore no better hold upon
your good opinion, I should expect some

credit for my motives from having undertaken to explain them to you at a moment
in which no dissimulation can avail me.
Which ever of the two mischiefs by which
this isle is frighted from her propriety shall
become prevalent, there is equally an end
of all the service you can receive from
men of my principles. The habits of our
whole lives have confirmed us so much in
enmity to both, that we must hope for as
little lenity from those they call jacobins,
as we receive from those by whom jacobinism is imputed to us. As we still think,
and mean, while we have the power, to act
upon the persuasion, that between *jacobinism,* (as the phrase runs, and the system of
those who have undertaken to cure it,
there is a medium, and that medium our
constitution, proscription and persecution
are the mildest destinies that await us from
either. By the first of these factions we
are called the advocates of slavery: the
second already prepares its fire and faggot
to cure us of republicanism. All this is in
order. Let me add, such are precisely the
sort of accusations, I would wish to come
from such quarters. From me therefore,
as they deter me from no duty, they shall
draw no complaint. Who indeed, from
such adversaries ever hopes for plain dealing? Why should I expect that Ministers,
with whom we are first at issue on a ques-

tion of immediate preservation, would depart from their usual practice, and discover towards men who think as I do, any of the mercy of a fair and liberal hostility? To desist from misrepresentation were to confess themselves conquered. At present it is some proof of spirit, at least among those who have taste to admire such ministers, that misfortunes which have bowed down the pride of their country, possess no power over the stubborn malice of their defamation, or lower their tone to one single sentiment of truth or reason. Who shall undertake for such men that they will learn moderation from adversity? They over whose heads the American war has passed without instructing them in any thing but the tricks by which wars are supported, may well calculate upon putting off the hour of repentance and retribution. These are the spoiled children of a credulous dotard people who encourage their froward malice to rail at and scold at their pleasure all the old faithful servants of the mansion. But we shall receive our dismission from no hands but your's: we shall take none of their insolent warnings, or leave them to the bent of their own mischevious inclinations. Then let them call *jacobin* till the very echo is hoarse.

Do me the justice to believe, that if I have so long deferred submitting these matters to you, as certainly it was known to me long ago that we had ceased to think alike upon publick affairs, I have been actuated neither by disregard to your wishes, nor by any desire of shunning enquiry. All of you remember and lament the separation of the Whig party. With no means of averting that misfortune beyond the influence of my individual voice, it happened to me to be near enough to witness the origin of many of those measures which brought it about. Yet although withheld from participating in them by a mixed sentiment of regret and distaste, I could not avoid taking my share, as a servant of the publick, in the consequences to which they led. Thus circumstanced, and knowing that the justification of ourselves is often mistaken for an attack on those who differ from us, I carefully abstained from any step which might tend to throw impediment in the way of conciliation. While there was a chance that time, reason, the magnitude of events, and the impending dangers of our country, could heal our divisions, and bring men, in spite of artifice and refinement, to act upon some acknowledged view of our situation, I was willing to let matters quietly take their course, and risque my vindication with you upon the general settlement of our party differences with each other. Long, therefore, did I watch their progress, in mute restraint and painful expectation. That period is passed. Nothing now remains but to perform the last sad offices, and give to the grave all the fond hopes with which our long union and consistency had inspired me. Released from this sweet bondage, ill exchanged for the barren freedom of individuality, I can now fully go into the particulars of my conduct during three years of as sharp and trying difficulty as it ever fell to the lot of man to struggle with. What that conduct is, how it accords with that which preceded it, what promise it offers for the future, if the future shall yet be ours, these are questions which I can now desire you to sift, and probe to the bottom, with as little fear for others as I ever entertained for myself. Not that I can yet promise to trace with a steady hand the story of our unfortunate divisions. Who that remembers the proud party assembled under the auspices of the marquis of Rockingham, and whose object it was to form a balance against even the crown itself in favour of the people, and the popular part of our constitution---who that has to boast a share in its immortal acts, can contemplate without sorrow, or describe without shame, the spectacle of ruin and degradation it now exhibits; dispersed and dishonoured,---its chiefs in hopeless bondage to the power they had combined to limit, and that haughty instrument of its will from whose hands they would have torn its symbols? For one, I am wholly unfit for this task. I cannot begin a fresh conflict while the wounds are yet green which were dealt me in the last, from little less than a brother's hand. I think that I know as well as any man what it is to act from a sense of duty. Severe and inflexible, it forces us to keep our ground, and bear up against the public evils brought on by the ill considered measures often of our best friends. But more is not to be expected. Nature and our hearts are beyond its jurisdiction. Pardon, Sir, these infirmities, if such they are, and think not the worse of my defence if it spare them all reproach, and confine itself, as far as they may be concerned, to suggestions for their own prudence.

Indeed, with every sentiment of preference for the side I have chosen, I am not disposed to push my condemnation of others further than the circumstances themselves demand. You would not have me rake in the filth and mire of accusations which I have a thousand times reprobated when in the mouths of their worst enemies, for the sake of a discovery which, if true, must destroy all future confidence

in man, by degrading human nature in
some of its fairest examples. It is to my
shame, perhaps, but I own that my way
of feeling is quite the reverse. Instead of
searching for common places against the
former Whigs in the old magazines of
scurrility, first collected by the malignant
activity of their present associates, I confess that the separation from persons in
whose society I have passed a long and
toilsome period of life with little sense of
its cares, never recurs to me without renewing the most painful emotions. Possibly it is the size of this misfortune that im-
poses silence on all the fretful feelings
which beget complaint and its corresponding animosities. The great national adversity which this separation has brought
home to us, acts upon me as adversity
ought, by subjugating the minor passions
to its mighty law, and cleansing them from
the feculence of uncharitableness and revenge. No, Sir, it was not a paltry ea-
gerness for power, or place, which rent
asunder this generous combination of talents and virtues. Never shall the just
resentments of abjured friendship teach me
thus to calumniate the services of so many
trying years. The whole of their conduct
who have separated from us, (I speak with
the exception of a very few) originates in
a sincere, but in my opinion, ill-founded

alarm. I think by mistaking the proximity of their own description of danger, they mistook the nature and true species of our danger itself. In fact the point from which the two branches of our party diverged, was so near to the sentiments and principles of each, that many persons who have been able to contemplate without passion the events which brought it about, have wondered why it ever happened. It may sound somewhat paradoxical to those who look only to things as they find them---but to me it seems, and this aggravates the misfortune an hundred fold,---that we separated with no difference of principle, properly so called, under the influence of nothing corrupt or disreputable, and with every disposition in the world to keep together. Those causes which produce disunion among common men, in the common affairs of the world, were here supplied first, by a great and generally admitted pressure of circumstances, and secondly, by a system of well-contrived, methodized cunning, which called up by turns to its aid, with a dexterity scarcely credible even in the highest finisher of small frauds, the angry vehemence of some, the honest prejudices of others, and the fat, idiot imbecility of the people at large. Let me not be thought to lessen the importance of those points on which we differed.

D

Alas! the world is bearing bloody testimony to it at this hour. We owe to this strange, and perverted way of seeing the same subject, and the obstinate pursuit of the measures it has suggested, the miseries of a dreadful war, and the still increasing bitterness of our domestic dissentions. You will understand me therefore as speaking of the character of our differences when I venture to class them rather with those which are derived from considerations of policy and prudence, than with those which flow from opposing principle. Such I think you will find them to be in general. Wide, deep, irreconcileable in their present state, but in their origin so nice and narrow, as to be traceable to a co-incidence of principle, and in many things even to a similarity, as to means, in some of the most essential articles of national interest.

Yielding thus at last to a necessity I always acknowledged, of submitting to those who have, through me, an interest so immediate and particular in the public transactions, a full explanation of my share in them, I come to demand judgment at your hands. Impressed, however, with a sense of the extreme delicacy of this subject, as well as of its importance, since possibly the course of our future lives may receive its bent and

direction from our conduct now as explained by our motives, I cannot, Sir, think
of trusting this task out of my own hands.
As little can I undertake it for any one
else. I must beg you, therefore, to consider the sentiments you may meet with
here, as those for which I alone am responsible; and for that same reason, with
the exception of one single document, thus
put in my early claim to be bound by no
other. I am in doubt, however, whether
the piece alluded to can be stated as an exception. It is history. It is authority. It
rests upon the same foundation that en-
sures stability to doctrine, and obedience to
government itself. It is a memorial which
if every other title of its great author to ce-
lebrity were obliterated, would alone fix
that high character by one common suffrage
bestowed upon him in whatever corner of
the world his name is pronounced. Even
this sober age is not without its prophets;
but it is the triumph of reason that she is
copied by superstition. The latest posterity to which the story of this day shall
descend, will recognize that intuitive mind
with which he looked through the dark
times before him at a glance, and discerned
in their embryo the evils of which in vain
he warned mankind. Mr. Fox's letter to
his constituents was written in December,
1792. In stating the motives of his con-

duct on his three motions early in that session, his sagacity has traced an outline so clear and definite, that there is no flying off from it except by the denial of demonstrated truth. Taking, therefore, that document for my guide, and grounding upon it the whole of what I shall trouble you with in the way of exculpation, I desire no better than to go to trial upon the whole question of our present state; of the justice, necessity, and wisdom of this war; of its effect upon your national honour; and of the security your government derives from it, and from the system of administration which it has created.

That which I find has been chiefly reproached to me by some of my most valuable friends, is an inconsistency, as they call it, between my known opinions both with regard to foreign policy, and our domestic government, and my conduct in Parliament of late whenever these subjects have come under discussion. They think, it seems, that a man so antigallican as I, one who so much reprobates both the crimes and the principles on which France has established her republic, and who confesses himself so much alarmed at her victories, should have given his support to the war quite as a thing of course. They profess to be as much surprised that, with my notions about reforms of parliament, and other popular topics, I should have opposed any of those measures which ministers have adopted to discourage them. While these impressions have gained ground against me in some quarters, a very different language is held in others. Little credit is given to my opposition by persons who, mistaking the whole spirit of that in which my principles have engaged me, conceive that it ought necessarily to have embraced all those circumstances of accident which help to captivate light and giddy minds. How can he be sincere, it is asked, in his dislike of this war, who sticks to the notions of the old school, and in spite of the revolution which philosophy has accomplished in France, feeds and nurses up his ancient prejudices against her power, and jealousy of her ambition? Of what value are those pretensions to patriotism, which instead of keeping pace with the discoveries of an enlightened age, obstinately reject all invitation to improvement, and although equally detesting persecution, assist its advocates to discountenance every rising effort of liberty? Assailed in this manner by both sides, and pressed by each alike with the nature and urgency of the times, I have yet been hardy enough to persevere in a middle course. The result is what I have expected. No one is content. Really, Sir, under a full conviction of having done the best for

your service, I cannot discommend the
zeal with which men, living as you do at a
distance from the scene, are apt to canvass
these sort of questions. I do feel that there
is much to be said in excuse for those, who
calling out in such a moment for decision,
which they are unable to see in any thing
that looks like an endeavour to preserve a
medium, have reproached me on some occasions with fear, at others with much
worse. I have long observed that it is
with the greatest difficulty you ever acquire
a knowledge of the commonest facts. For
the opinions of our parliamentary leaders,
your very best authority is a news-paper.
Opinions arising from facts, you are not
likely therefore to hear at any time; but
when you reflect upon the sort of transactions which are passing our doors every
day, and the corresponding, commensurate
opinions they must necessarily beget, to
what a distance are you not thrown in
every attempt to come at unadulterated
truth? Indeed, I scarcely know how truth
is to get to you. All ordinary methods of
conveying a full idea of our situation since
France has become the leading topic, must
fall infinitely short of it. You can learn it
by no statement of facts alone, however
faithfully detailed. That situation, I fear,
is too nearly connected with our passions!
These you must have the means of develop-

ing and combining with facts before the clouds which obscure your sight can effectually be dispersed. You must travel back with me a great way to reach the true origin of our misfortunes; back to the sessions of 1791, and to that day, ever to be marked with a black stone, on which Mr. Burke declared in parliament his final separation from Mr. Fox.

That was, indeed, a day of mourning to the Whig cause. Then began to rush in upon us, through the yawning chasm left by this convulsion in our system, the full tide of those waters of bitterness of which we have so largely tasted. The more I reflect upon this event, the more am I inclined to refer the whole of our present misfortunes to that first variance in our party. A very superficial view of public affairs since the close of the war with America, will be sufficient to shew the vast influence which these two celebrated men have possessed over the conduct of government. Authority has great weight with the people of this country; trick and contrivance go a considerable way; corruption almost every where is welcome; and all things considered, government, in times of peace, is, in all its practical parts, a tolerably easy task among us. But still something is wanted for shew. With all these facilities, we require a pretext. I

know there are many ways of depriving
talents and integrity of their proper ascendancy ; and perhaps it is true, what is often
reproached to us, that the most eloquent
speech in parliament never gains an additional vote. Yet with all these bad propen-
sities, enough remains of the popular spirit
of our government to ensure to eloquence
and distinguished abilities a degree of influence on the general conduct of affairs,
sufficient to operate, surely, although im-
perceptibly, great public benefits. The
treasures that are scattered are rarely lost.
If sometimes they are thrown before swine,
and trodden down in the mire, they are
not unfrequently gathered up by the pro-
vident foresight of the minister himself,
and thus brought into circulation by a
shorter cut. Whoever has taken the pains
to study the two great men of whom I am
speaking, must have observed the truth of
this. It cannot have escaped him that notwithstanding their proscription from court,
and those official situations which give the
immediate means of service, they had in
their union, even under circumstances of
considerable popular odium, often discon-
certed and held in check the wild projects, and wasteful phrenzy of its ministers.
They led the opinion of the country often
against its knowledge, always against its
will. Such for many years was their joint

efficacy and force; but not until that evil hour which called them forth in opposition to each other, was properly seen the whole compass of their mighty powers. Very early in the French revolution we that were the nearest began to tremble at their giant play. I think it was about the beginning of the year 1790, that an observation of Mr. Fox on the conduct of the French soldiery in a riot at Paris, drew from Mr. Burke some very severe strictures upon the leaders of that revolution. From that moment the question was thrown open to disputants of all sides: and here were discovered the first symptoms of a difference which was soon to shake society to its centre. It could be no less. Men of their size could not break company without dividing the world between them. The party they belonged to was not to be dissolved like a partnership in trade; neither could they, or either of them, quit that party, without risquing its destruction, and with that, the destruction of those public objects which it embraced. These lordly oaks, the pride of the forest, had struck root into the constitution itself, and could not be torn from its bosom without loosening the whole earth around, and withering the lesser plants that flourished beneath their shade.

To lead in this great conflict of opinion formed no part of the ambition of Mr.

E

Pitt. Who talks of *his* sentiments upon the French revolution? Who ever heard them? Strange as you may think it, he who pretends to the chief office in the British councils, and to stand at the head of Europe in a war of opinions, never on this most interesting subject has ventured one single opinion himself, which, by any chance, has excited common curiosity. It was not possible however that the conduct of a man in his very eminent station could be a matter of indifference to the world. I do not censure him, Sir, for not taking a part at once, and declaring in favour of the French revolution *as an example.* Assuredly it was right to see what would come of it, before any thing similar should be recommended to us. I am no enthusiast in these matters. As far as I know of their first constitution my dislike to it is very great. But to leave France to the trial of her experiment, was always in the power of an honest politician, and I think would have been the choice of a wise one. If they who governed the British councils had been disposed to act in the fair, *bona fide* meaning of such a determination, they would have discovered no shyness of speaking to foreign nations, in firm and becoming language, their sense, not of the experiment, but of the effort. This was the utmost that could be required of any mi.

nister; but so much, let me add, was required from any man holding that office
with the views of a statesman. Unhappily
Mr. Pitt had another use for it. If no opinions of his were worth a dispute, his interests were not a little concerned in pro-
moting the disputes of others. What sig-
nified it to such a first lord of the treasury,
busied as he was with his revenue regulations and details, whether France should
succeed or perish in the attempt to limit
her monarchy? This was a point he left to
be settled among his adversaries. They
differed. So much the better. The time
would soon come which by making him
the arbiter of their differences, must necessarily leave him the master of their fate.
Sensible of the vantage ground he occupied, and that it was one from which he
should be able, in any crisis, to guide the
current of men's opinions just into what
channel he pleased, he found himself deriving strength as a minister from that very
circumstance which took away all consideration from him as a politician. By the
part he should adopt, when a part was to
be adopted at all, he found himself enabled
to decide on no less a question than the
existence of the country, connected with
the perpetuity of his own power. To give
away such an advantage for the barren
purpose of doing good, never was dreamt

of in his philosophy. A great party in the House of Commons had long opposed his measures, condemned the principle of his appointment to office, and denied all credit or character to his administration. It was his first policy to break that party. He waited therefore to see to what extent the differences recently declared between the two chief persons in it would go, what objects and what men they would embrace, and how they were likely to be promoted by the importance, and the growing pressure of affairs themselves.

These three persons therefore, Mr. Burke, Mr. Fox, and Mr. Pitt, the two first distinguished by their renown, the third by his unbounded power, may be considered as laying at that time the foundations of three systems for the conduct of Great Britain, with distinct and very opposite views. What might have ensued from adopting either of those recommended by Mr. Burke, or Mr. Fox, no man, as they have never been tried, will pronounce. To that of Mr. Fox none of you would listen; and all the means of giving effect to Mr. Burke's, have been squandered upon the minister's experiment. To this therefore, I shall direct my chief enquiry; and must request a few moments of your attention to a short, and compressed narrative of some of the leading events which intervened

between the debate on the Quebec bill, and
the sudden meeting of parliament in December 1792; in order to exhibit to you
those causes, drawn from a mixed view of
domestic and foreign affairs during that
period, through which the country was en-
trapped into the unexplained, discretionary
system of Mr. Pitt, to the exclusion of the
other two, and by which it has been precipitated into its present situation of unex-
ampled calamity and disgrace.

To begin with your foreign affairs. From
one cause or other not necessary to detail
in this place, Europe, at the first of these
periods, was in a situation of very considerable embarassment. The Minister, by his
restless intrigues, had successively stirred
up a war against the Empress of Russia on
the side of the Porte and Sweden, and a
rebellion against the Emperor in the Austrian Netherlands. That spirit of disaffection which he had universally excited
against the Austrian government, by means
of Vandernoot and Van Eupen, a disaffection which in its consequences has visited Europe with the severest calamity it
ever knew, which has twice thrown those
rich provinces into the hands of France,
and given her, it is to be feared, perpetual
possession of Holland, had drawn off the
Emperor from the Russian alliance. In
the expectation from this event, of com-

pelling the Czarina to accept what terms
he pleased, his vanity had dictated to her
the conditions of a peace with the Turks,
and his folly was preparing to enforce
them. The result was far from flattering.
The Empress of Russia rejected his pro-
posals, laughed at his menace, and defied
his power. To engage her to some concessions which might have the appearance
of a salvo to his own honour, as soon as
the session was closed he dispatched a minister to St. Petersburg, whose abilities,
undoubtedly, were equal to any task,
and whose character in settling the terms
of pacification, if they should be unfavour-
able, might afford some protection to his
own. The whole summer, however, was
consumed in fruitless negociations. He
had failed to bully; he was content to submit; and there was an end of the question.
No sooner was this difference concluded
than an object of higher interest arose, and
the affairs of France began to occupy the
cabinets of Europe. The situation of the
royal family at Paris quickened the tardy
conferences at Pillnitz. Of these, the general result is tolerably well known. It is
true that no final determination was come
to between the German powers, *at that
time*, to interfere by force in the affairs of
France. The fact is, and the advocates
for these princes are welcome to the whole

benefit of it, that the determination was
provisional, and left intirely to the accession of the King of Great Britain. They
not only thought that an honest neutrality
on our parts would be fatal to such a purpose, but that without our active co-operation the enterprise itself was impracticable.
But the coyness of our cabinet, whose first
Minister was covering his head with shame
for his recent disgrace, deferred the execu-
tion of this rash project. In the then feelings of the British nation no man could
expect to be heard to the end of his speech
who should propose to disturb France in
the settlement of her constitution. Before
Mr. Pitt could consent to stir a step towards such a measure, it was necessary
that it should appear to originate with the
country, and not to have been planned in
the closet; and that the public opinion
should be so distinctly pronounced, as not
only to leave him without any immediate
fear of losing his place, but to afford
him, in every point of view, an exemp-
tion from all future responsibility.

These happy circumstances which enabled him to preserve a decent exterior towards France almost without the trouble of
professing neutrality, had the further use
of helping him to keep back any decisive
declarations in parliament, the effect of
which might bring the disputes among his

opponents to a point before they were ripe
for his full purpose. It was not worth his
while, for the sake of a few individuals,
however considerable in rank and character, to risque a proceeding which by throwing the whole country at once on the side
of Mr. Fox, might on the one hand, dimi-
nish considerably the extent of our party
differences, and render those which had
taken place of no benefit to him, on the
other. Our first meeting in February,
1792, must have fully confirmed these impressions. He could not avoid seeing how
strongly the publick opinion was against
engaging in any such confederacy as that
which had been projected at Pillnitz. Domestic affairs, and the interests of our own
government, seemed to have a more pressing claim upon us. That same House of
Commons which had pledged itself to support the extravagant measure of a war with
Russia for the restoration of her conquests
upon the Dniester, now unblushingly trans-
ferred its applause to the pusillanimous surrender of that object. That same House
of Commons, upon the statement of certain
corrupt practices at an election for Westminster, committed by a secretary to the
treasury, and which looked very like a
fraud upon the revenue, refused all enquiry
into his conduct. Practices of this nature,
not only tolerated but justified on the part

of government, began about this time to provoke a species of censure, novel in its kind, and wholly distinct from that with which they were met by the regular opposition. The writings of Paine had been eagerly circulated. These condemned in the lump the whole system of our government. They held up the theory of it as false, and the practice as pernicious. Little managed as were the terms in which they spoke of monarchy and aristocracy, the object of their chief hostility seemed to be the House of Commons. Just at this moment, and in the plenitude of their popular currency, before the sober understandings of the people could recover from its first impulse, and detect the mischief lurking beneath the false but plausible doctrines contained in these writings, the House of Commons, to screen the imbecility of one minister, and the corruption of another, is made to exhibit in its own conduct an illustration of the worst, and most dangerous of them all. It occurred also to some gentlemen who acted with us, that the conduct of administration was not all we had to complain of. They thought that these practices began materially to affect the credit and character of government itself. They thought that no remedy remained for this growing evil, but by procuring a reform in the representation of the people, and pas-

F

sing a bill for short parliaments. Sensible
at the same time of the mischief, it was
their wish to avert the danger, of the new
theories, ᵇ producing some moderate
plan, wʰ ⸍ limiting and fixing the
public ⸱ ⸱ion, should frustrate all
hope ᴄ ⸱ ⸱g men from their first duty,
and giʋⸯⸯ ᵹ them a taste for desperate experiments upon their constitution. These
gentlemen, although certainly without con-
sulting such of the party as they knew to
be adverse to the measure, imagined, it is
probable, that in bringing it forward under
the then circumstances, they gave no
grounds for a schism beyond what existed
upon former occasions, when it had been
discussed. At all events they conceived so
much higher of the importance of their own
scheme than of the necessity of preserving
the union and consistency of the Whig
party, that they resolved upon the trial,
and prepared every thing to give it its utmost effect.

Under these impressions they determined
against any mode of bringing it forward in
their capacities as individuals. They associated as a party. They gave themselves a party designation, and entered
into party engagements; and in order more
thoroughly to obtain the sanction of the
country to their proceedings, they gave
notice in the month of May, of this year,

of their intention to introduce it early in the ensuing sessions.

If these gentlemen ever imagined that a step so important in its nature could pass by without provoking, from those who had ever resisted what is called the reform of parliament, a most determined opposition, the event soon proved how much they were mistaken. For myself I must acknowledge, that, with the fullest belief in the good intentions of its immediate promoters, I could not see without the deepest regret, the party with which I acted, and which I deemed fully competent in its professions to *every* branch of the public service, diminished by the secession of those who appeared ready in this manner, to sacrifice every thing to their own scheme. But there were others, of infinitely more weight, who in addition to their old objections, were alarmed at the complexion of the times. They argued that the example of France could not be without its consequences upon the minds of Englishmen, that the question of reform must necessarily connect itself in the discussion with the proceedings which had there taken place; that while the question was of a remote, and speculative nature, the agitation of it was comparatively harmless, but brought so near to practice and experiment as it now appeared to be, it grew far more serious, and demanded from those

who disliked it, a degree of resistance pro-
portionate to its probability of success.
They saw, under these impressions, great
additional aid afforded it by the means of
a party embodied for its prosecution, and
they knew no better method of defeating
it than by concert and combination with
its enemies. What they thought right, they
soon resolved to make effective. A mes-
sage from his Majesty to the duke of Portland produced an interview with Mr. Pitt,
in which it was agreed to check the mischiefs apprehended, by a proclamation
against seditious writings.

It was probably less to suppress these
writings than to shew the weight of that influence with which it was determined to resist their effects, that they chose a measure
of this general nature which went to nothing more, at that time, than the accidental circumstances of danger with which
they thought the question of reform to be
connected. Unfortunately however our
debates which turned upon so many important points of domestic government,
and now began to embrace those of an extended foreign policy, could not be carried
on in this adverse manner between the parties who had set them on foot, without engaging to a considerable degree their passions. The society of the Friends of the
People complained that this proclamation,

although in terms levelled against the writings of Paine, was in truth and effect,
aimed at them. The duke of Portland and
his friends recriminated, by urging the circumstances of hostility towards them, and
their objects, which had marked the formation of the society. The proclamation, it
was alledged, was temporary, and depend-
ent upon the circumstances of danger;
whereas the declaration to which the society
had pledged itself, held up a permanent
object, to be pursued at all hazards, and
enforced by every means. Thus originated
a train of evils which circumstances soon
rendered incurable. The leaders of this
society, rejecting all manner of compromise, which in justice to the duke of Portland I must say was offered them, declared
their determination to persevere. Those
who concurred in the proclamation were
equally resolved to follow it up by that system of measures to which it seemed obviously to point. Between the two, the
real, solid, unchangeable interests of the
Whig cause fell to the ground, and were
forgotten for ever.

You see, Sir, that even if the war between France and the German powers had
not broke out, which it did about this time,
the opinions of Mr. Burke and Mr. Fox,
with respect to France, could no longer
have remained the subject of a mere spe-

culative difference. Every thing began to
partake of it. The transactions of that
country were become gradually interwoven
with all the domestic concerns of our own.
There was a French taste, sweet or bitter,
in the food we took for our daily nourish-
ment. How could it be otherwise, when
Europe all around us was in arms, when
it was known that the British court was
heart and soul in the confederacy, and that
she was only restrained from declaring herself by doubts, which speedily would be
done away, with regard to the dispositions
of the people at large? Such was the hu-
mour in which we reached the end of our
first sessions of 1792. It finished just as
Mr. Pitt could desire for his individual interests. These every day were gaining fresh
life and vigour from the public embarrassments. If he had not succeeded in totally
dissolving the Whig union, he had at least
effected that which made it as much as we
could do to keep together. The breach
between Mr. Burke and Mr. Fox was
widened, not only by the encreasing interest which every man felt in French affairs,
but by the new matter which had arisen
out of the discussions I have been alluding
to, and the new men whom they comprised.
To push these dissentions still further, or
at least to find out how far they had ac-
tually carried us, Mr. Pitt, during the sum-

mer, opened, through the medium of the
present chancellor, a sort of negociation
for a change in the ministry, with some of
the leaders of the old opposition. What
were its pretended objects, why it failed,
who were purchased by his offers, or who
duped by his duplicity, are questions not
immediately within my purpose to investigate. Enough is apparent to shew you that
he lost nothing by the attempt. Though
defeated for the present, and in some respects disgraced, he could always renew it
while the French revolution wore an as-
pect which might be thought menacing to
this country, and the Friends of the People pursued the objects of their association. Circumstances might enable him
to succeed better another time. Events
of great and pressing importance were fast
approaching. On the 10th of August the
jacobin party at Paris deposed and im-
prisoned the unhappy Louis. Such an act
to a Minister with Mr. Pitt's views, however desirable at some distance, must have
come rather too soon. It seemed difficult
to put off any longer some declaration of
the sentiments of the British court; and
yet it was evident, notwithstanding the
horrible massacres at the prisons which
followed the 10th of August, that a very
small proportion of considerable persons
in England, and none, absolutely none at

all of the great mass of the people, was disposed to declare war. In this dilemma Mr. Pitt, like all men who play a little game in great emergencies, did the very worst thing that could be done. He re-called Lord Gower from Paris, leaving a pacific declaration towards the provisional executive government established there. To deceive the royalists, he took a step al-ways in modern times regarded as a decla-ration of war. To deceive the rest of mankind he engaged himself to France through the very executive council which afterwards he refused to recognize, for the maintenance of a strict neutrality. He did that which by being amicable in words and hostile in fact, left him at full liberty to pursue his double game until he could sound the dispositions of parties in En-gland and put the alternative of war, or peace, home to them, before he should an-swer it himself. Fortunately for his pro-jects this very revolution of the 10th of August was chosen by some vain societies in England for the subject of a vote, and an address of felicitation to the national assembly. New food for alarm! new ar-guments for supporting the ministry! Meanwhile the eyes of mankind were turn-ed towards the march of the combined for-ces to Paris. All controversy was sus-pended; Every interest seemed attached to

the success or failure of that expedition;
until the retreat from Champagne, and the
victories of the French in the Netherlands,
gave a bolder tone to the language of the
reforming societies, and brought out into
broad day the large views by which many
persons in them began to be actuated.

To keep these transactions any longer
from pressing forward into our debates,
seemed just as little possible as it was to
debate them without hostility. With differences of principle comparatively slight,
those that began to prevail with respect to
the mode, and degree in which Great Britain ought to take part in the affairs of the
continent, grew every day more extensive.
France had disgusted the world by her cruelties, and alarmed it by her ambition. To
temporize with the one, or to bend to
the other, entered as little into the views
of the great leader of opposition, as it
did into those of any set of men his Majesty could have chosen for his advisers. Yet with every sentiment which
bespoke resolution in the substance, he
felt every possible scruple about the
mode; as he foresaw that it was precisely
upon this mode that the whole justice of
the question would hereafter be found to
turn, and that it would be seen whether we
had interfered with an intent to restrain
her ambition and aggrandizement, or to

G

change her government and punish her crimes. He thought, therefore, that it was necessary to interfere, he thought that it would be right to arm, but above all things that it was indispensable to negociate. This way, which he professed to be his, of viewing the subject, totally, as you will observe, excluded from the consideration of it all that set of reasons, in favour of war, connected either with our own government or with that of France, which weighed so considerably with other gentlemen. In the opinions of this latter description the destruction, or dismemberment of the republic was the best method of repressing the violence of the reforming societies in Great Britain, and little difficulty remained, with them, as to the mode of declaring war against France, so long as they could secure the co-operation of the other branches of the confederacy.

Here was an opening the minister could not miss. But the blow was to be struck at once, and suddenly. Delay might bring on explanation, and explanation would ruin all. Early therefore in the December of this year he issued a Proclamation calling Parliament together on the 13th, under the pretence of actual plots and insurrections. Steadfastly keeping an eye on our main difference, a speech was framed for his Majesty with a view to the closely inter-

weaving together, and by a solemn public
instrument making one cause of, the dangers
apprehended from the reforming societies,
and the transactions going on in France
and upon the continent. This speech and
the address upon it was to prepare the
ground for a set of measures founded upon
these dangers, with which the Duke of
Portland and those who thought with him
were sure ultimately to fall in. It was to
give the Minister this security for his place,
namely, that it would be the means of bringing the divisions of our party to a point
before he should give any decisive pledge
to the public, as to the measures he meant
to pursue in that momentous emergency.
There was yet some difficulty in settling
the language of this speech. If the Minister should declare for war, without first as-
certaining what support he was to expect,
he risqued his present power. If he should
continue *fairly* neutral, he risqued all the
expected benefits of our disunion. What
therefore he found it safest to determine
upon, was a neutrality which should be just
enough to save appearances with the public, but which could not in its nature deceive the penetrating eye of Mr. Burke.
With the one, he obtained the credit of doing all he could to avoid that war which
the other saw with satisfaction must inevitably follow from the conduct he then pur-

sued, unless some very sudden and sensible alteration should take place in it.

To keep him up stoutly to this point seemed the chief aim of that division of our party, which began about this time to announce its separation from us, by some high language in the House of Commons, and by associations and engagements entered into with other persons in the spirit of direct hostility to the old principle of our union. No sacrifice was deemed too great to win from his wary policy any assent, however cold, to the measures they were projecting. Whatever his most vigilant jealousy could exact in the way of full security for his place, all that could be asked as preliminary abdications of the great constitutional points on which they had been at issue with him for so many years, every reproach they had uttered against his integrity and capacity, every claim upon their steadiness that private honour or friendship could urge, all, all was thrown in one undistinguished heap at his feet in this frantic fit of zeal and fury. Now began to display itself the dexterity with which he had conducted this whole intrigue. While in truth he had been courting, and coquetting with them every day since the proclamation against seditious writings had announced their growing loves to the world, by putting them under the necessity of taking the first open step, it seemed as if they were courting him, and pressing him to precipitate matters with France against his more sober judgment. It was a circumstance, trivial to all appearance but which came very much in aid of his views, that his seat in parliament had become vacant by his acceptance of the Cinque ports. His absence for his re-election left Mr. Burke in possession of the House of Commons during the three first days of the most important period in which parliament had met for a century. Assembling as we did under the impressions which that gentleman's speeches and writings had produced, and which the minister's violent measure of convoking us had sanctioned, a great majority saw with Mr. Burke's eyes, felt with his passions, and followed his cry to arms with an ardour and enthusiasm little inferior to his own. The Minister on his return found the whole business done to his hand; and all of it the work of his enemies. A violent war spirit was raised which he could either quicken or retard just as it should suit his own purpose. On all sides he was safe. His was the past, the present, and the future. Hymns of triumph, and crowns of victory awaited him for his final conquest over the Whigs. The public praised his moderation, and the whole responsibility of the war was thrown upon the shoulders of Mr. Burke and his friends.

Such, Sir, was our meeting on the 13th
of December, 1792. In this short but
faithful narrative, I have as yet said nothing of my own conduct. The facts are
now before you on which you must judge
of it. The first head of charge against me
relates to the Friends of the People, and
through them, connects itself with that of
encouraging the other societies whose proceedings have been so justly and generally
reprobated. This charge, as against me,
is untenable in any one of its parts. It pro-
ceeds upon a supposition, that these gentlemen and their society were so highly fa-
voured as to produce a considerable degree
of assimilation between them, and the future views of the party, and a consequent
departure from its original objects. Names
of high authority were whispered about as
countenancing this institution, and encouraging its proceedings. Enemies and friends
dispersed these rumours. From the one
they came in the shape of charge and accu-
sation, enforced by the aid of publications
universally disseminated; from the other, in
that of self-congratulation and triumph at
the acquisition of such support, and by way
of encouragement to proselytes. At this time
of day it were fighting with a shadow to
expose the idleness of these rumours.
Even when they were generally current, I
thought the only notice they were worth,

was to send you a list of the names of this so terrible club. The sort of denial, however, which I found was expected from me, went to more serious lengths. It was asked why I did not concur in the measures then projected, or in other words, why I did not join the minister, against them? Sir, I shall never repent the not giving you by my versatility, this proof of my attachment to old principles. I can never think the worse of myself for the sort of rusty obstinacy I had contracted from having been out upon your service in all weathers, and which kept me from veering about with every gale which sprung up from Freemason's Tavern. Certainly I disapproved what was doing there; Indeed, at that very time I determined, (nor am I likely to change this resolution) never to become a member of a party in which their influence should preponderate. But was there no keeping to this without joining Mr. Pitt? Or was there, after all, and admitting this society to have had the worst views, any comparison to be made between it, and him, as to their respective powers for working mischief? Was I to forget this minister's early enmity to the marquis of Rockingham, his uniform endeavours to destroy the Whigs, his total disdain of all publick principle, his incapacity for government? Was all to be forgiven him, and the wrongs he had done the constitution during an administration of nine years, at once to be wiped away, merely because a set of gentlemen had thought proper to bring forward the question of reform at a bad time, and in a new and objectionable shape? I have much respect, and very partial feelings for many individuals of that society: I see nothing very formidable in Mr. Pitt's abilities: But really, Sir, weighing this question as a choice between evils, I could not possibly consent to rate them so high, or him so low. The consolidation of his absolute independent power, seemed to me the worst death the constitution could suffer. I speak as an anti-reformer. In joining Mr. Pitt, independent of all its other evils, there was not even a prospect of security to us for any length of time, from the very same dangers we so much dreaded from other quarters. There was no reciprocity in his treaty. We were asked to give up, for ever, the principle of our opposition to him, on his agreeing to resist the reform for a time determinable at his own pleasure. We were urged to draw a sponge over all the crimes he had perpetrated to come at power and to keep it, because about 20 members of the House of Commons were going to try, in the year 1793, what we had no promise from him that he would not try himself in the year 1794. For this

temporary aid which we did not want, as
we were strong enough to defeat the measure whether he acted with us, or not, we
were to surrender up all the great purposes
for which the Whigs, since the days of
Charles the Second, had held up a monarchy of King, Lords, and Commons, as
the best of human contrivances to connect
liberty with government; and we were to
take from his lips, and thenceforward to
act upon, the law which in his omnipo-
tence he had pronounced in 1784, upon the
true nature, and balance of these powers.
To me, the alternative was of no difficulty.
It was too much, I thought, to put the
honour of the House of Commons, and
with that the whole of its value as a
controul over factious mobs, and factious
ministers, into the hands of a man only
known to us by his endeavours to destroy
its best functions. It was telling me just
nothing, to say that he had thrown off his
early confidences, and left the first instru-
ments of his power to their fate, when
every action of his life discovered so close
an understanding with them. All these
lures, thus artfully thrown out to decoy
the Whig aristocracy to his side, but ill
concealed from me the desperate adventurer who but the other day, as it were,
collecting together a promiscuous horde
from St. James's and St. Giles's, had

H

stretched his desolating hand over the fairest portion of our inheritance. I could not consent with Mr. Windham and others, to call in a professed foreign enemy, in hopes of converting him into an auxiliary, and bribing him to defend one half of the constitution by the sacrifice of the other. We knew Mr. Pitt only as an invader. Like his Vandal predecessors, I thought that the exposure of our treasures would tempt his rapacity more than it would gain his friendship. I deprecated these coward capitulations, of lazy, luxurious wealth, this wretched barter of gold for iron, as equally unbecoming our wisdom and our honour. Would to God that Mr. Windham and the gentlemen who followed him had recollected the never varying destiny of those who call in the aid of allies more powerful than themselves. But the bands of reason already were broken asunder. The spirit of strange fancies was abroad. Airy forms of mischief flitted before their eyes at every step they took in this vale of terrors; until harrassed, and hunted into madness by their own shadows, they fell within the magic circle of the sorcerer, where they slumber in the nullity, but not the repose, of death.

You have here the precise degree of my participation in the transactions of the Friends of the People. Of any direct con-

cern in those of other societies, I have
never been accused at all. Indeed the
whole set of charges brought against me,
is of a nature to afford me much consolation. It is surely flattering to have it thus
publickly acknowledged by very acute political adversaries, that they have not been
able to reproach me with one single act of
venality or corruption. Their whole force
is strained to make out a connection with a
society whose measures had a supposed
tendency to encourage bad designs in
others. After all their sophisticating scan-
dals, this is the sum total of a charge which
was to degrade me from the rank I had
won after so many years of service, to
turn me adrift upon a treacherous and in-
hospitable element, and in the eyes of men
like you, to sink me into a fellowship of
guilt with the drinkers of blood in France,
and the rhapsodising mimicks of their
crimes in England!

To exculpate myself from tolerating what
were nick-named " French principles," and
from favouring their progress in Europe by
the acquiescence of the British nation, was
another ground on which you reckoned
upon my support to ministers at the commencement of this session. First I must
remark that it is with me, a great proof of the
insincerity of these ministers, that in such
a fearful crisis instead of doing any one act

which bore the appearance of conciliating the divided sentiments of their country, their chief study was to produce a case to the statement of which no man who had opposed them upon system could assent without dishonouring himself. The footing on which they put this claim of assistance from Mr. Fox and his friends, was one which if acceeded to by him, included the confession that he had so conducted himself as to make it necessary that he should be purged of certain crimes imputed to him by giving some proof, which they suppose he never had given, of his zeal for the constitution, and for the liberties of Europe. Before he could enter into a course of good citizenship, it was necessary that he should begin by acknowledging that he had been a bad citizen all his life. Such claims, from such men, could not be listened to without indignation. They knew it themselves. They had brought them forward to be rejected, and in order to build upon their rejection a set of charges against us, adapted to the popular taste which enjoys calumny, and the popular fears which exult in persecution. But if honour opposed these concessions, reason forbade them. Whatever had been the crimes, or the triumphs of France, the measures of administration were only calculated to encrease and provoke them, and to render the safety of Europe yet more precarious. I did not support him, because he set out upon a confused principle, unjust as far as it could be understood, and leading to a war which his conduct every day proves to have been unnecessary. I did not support him, because with a party view, he mixed up his schemes on France with contrivances at home in regard to dangers which he, as well as I, knew to be false. This, Sir, was an error, to say no worse of it, in the outset, which admitted of no remedy short of taking the administration entirely out of his hands. In answer therefore to those, who, with a view of introducing by a side wind a charge against me of partiality towards France, accuse me of a slow sense to our danger, I think you will collect, from what I have just stated, that I met my colleagues to the full as much alive to what was real in it as any man of them. What indeed but alarm could our situation both foreign and domestic inspire? France was to be resisted. What were our means? Was it enough that we had a liberal parliament and a loyal people? Was ability, temper, courage, in those who were to preside over the government to count for nothing? Was this precisely the moment in which, exchanging our experience for our hopes, it became wise to speculate that ignorance, imbecil-

lity, and presumption, to work all the good
effects of their opposite virtues, required
only to be indulged in the full swing of
their own discretion, exempt from all
check or controul of any kind? Is this a
true picture? Who doubts it? Assuredly
not they who made these qualities in our
cabinet the inducement for their joining it.
Sir, that cabinet was every where, and in
every way, contemptible. Its character
abroad was that of a set of inconsiderate,
troublesome, mischief-makers, without capacity to understand the complicated interests of Europe, steadiness to adhere to their
engagements, or resolution to execute their
objects. At home, what we had predicted
of them in the year 1784, and above all,
their inadequacy to make government res-
pected, was daily verifying both by their
own confessed nullity in the season of such
mighty danger, and the absence of all public opinion, expectation, and character
from their counsels. This was the cabinet,
so acknowledged by all, so described by
many even in the honey moments of their
virgin vows, which I was to assist in defe-
cating and purging by a course of moral
quackery handed up to me from a school
of mountebank metaphysics, whose disci-
ples profess to cure the distemper by means
of the distemper itself; and who on a
scheme of logic well worthy of their other

pretensions, argue that the more you increase its present symptoms the more you provide for its ultimate extirpation. Like those *gratis* practitioners who cry about their poisons under the hackneyed invitation of " no cure, no pay," I was to join in persuading the public to swallow down this trash, as a remedy for all evils, under the ingenious pretence, truly, of affording Ministers a disinterested support. Sir, I had as little inclination, as the country had leisure, for these preposterous refinements. Our situation called for prompt decision, and vigorous action. That there had been great mismanagement somewhere, was a fact admitted. Looking about me to discover in what part our system was defective, my eyes beheld nothing in the main pillars of it that could inspire me with a wish for change. I saw a flourishing commerce, an ample revenue, justice well administered, a people rich, contented, and as adverse as I could wish them to the new experiments of the day. I saw at the same time a ministry generally acknowledged to be incompetent to the preservation of these advantages. Reasoning strait forward, it seemed to me that as we had found out the seat of the disorder, the obvious mode of treatment was to apply our remedies to the morbid part. I concluded that there could be no question between the value of such a ministry, and the most trifling hazard these advantages could be exposed to by keeping them. It struck me as scarcely admitting a dissenting opinion that this was the time for us to renew, and bring again before the public the substance of those resolutions which the Commons had passed in the year 1784. Nine years had been consumed by the Whig opposition in a state of proscription and disgrace for the part they had borne in those memorable votes. The day of proof was come at last. It was to be found in the actual state of the nation; in the security of its constitution; in the care taken for the preservation of its foreign interests; and in the splendour of its fame. But independent of all arguments from mere consistency, it was my firm persuasion that such an administration alone, as the Commons then contended for, could serve the country; because it was just the moment in which Europe expected from us not only a clear system, but those vigorous demonstrations which never can be made but by a ministry fairly representing the country, and understood to speak its sense. For let us not think we could have deceived Europe, if to deceive her had been our interest, by setting up that administration as the faithful representative of the national will. Foreign cabinets were not so ignorant of the state of our parties, as not to see that, for a length of years, there had been a systematick exclusion from office of all men, of whatever rank or services, who looked to power through any means except the private favour of a cabal at court; that this system of favouritism with all its attendant instabilities, had at length prevailed over the best practice of our ancestors; and that so far from having to deal with a strong, efficient state council, they had in truth no other security for the national faith pledged to them through such a government, than the word of a court as capricious as any of their own, and the character of a Minister who had betrayed, or bullied, or humbled himself before, almost every one of them in its turn. Very different, according to my apprehension, were the councils which were to give to Great Britain her proper form and station in any confederacy that she might have thought it expedient to accede to for the preservation of the liberties of Europe. Very different was the sort of leader she required to conduct her negociations, to wield her force, and to calm, with the authority of his name, the hostile and discordant elements of such a combination.

It was my opinion therefore, that instead of attempting the chimerical experiment of infusing any portion of wisdom or integrity into that set of ministers, an experiment

I

which in the first step towards its execu-
tion, involved the unequivocal sacrifice of
all that we had been contending for in your
name, it was our duty to get rid of them
by every effort of union and co-operation.
It was a case in which the attainment of
this great preliminary good, demanded, as
I thought, the sacrifice of differences ten
thousand times greater than any that had
hitherto subsisted among us as members of
a party. But if these sentiments were too
general to bind the conduct of a wise man
in the moment of consternation in which
we met, the circumstances under which
ministers called us together were such as
to leave no choice to those who disdained
participating in the most wicked act of de-
lusion that ever was practised upon the
credulity of mankind. Need I dwell on
the disgusting fables of conspiracies and
insurrections,--the fortifying of the tower,---
the contrived delay of all correspondence by
the stoppage of the mails, or lay open to
you the whole apparatus of political buf-
foonery as it was played off at one and the
same moment on the imaginations of ignorant men? The whole, in my mind, was a
wicked, and a most dangerous *trick*; since,
whether there existed any real cause for
alarm on other grounds, or no, the pretence of a plot when the ministers knew
that there was no plot, was sure to create

an alarm of its own, and to engage one part
of the kingdom (as too fatally the event has
proved) in a conspiracy against the peace,
the characters, and in some instances,
against the lives of the other. Yet this was
at least equalled by another evil with which
I thought the country threatened in some
warm speeches during this debate. His
Majesty, as it is known, had engaged for
the observance of a strict neutrality in the
affairs of France. Ill as I thought that neutrality either kept, or provided for, any
thing appeared better than the principle on
which a total departure from it was recommended. There was always a hope, before
the sword should be appealed to, that
Great Britain by her situation would have
been able to meditate a peace for Europe;
not a mere suspension of hostilities, but a
permanent pacification, which would have
sent France back to her ancient limits, and
the confederates to their homes; which
would have left that country to the settlement of her own laws, and the Princes of
Europe to salutary reflections on the im-
possibility of preventing it. I voted therefore, in compliance with these sentiments,
for Mr. Fox's amendment on the first day
of this stormy session. I voted afterwards
for the motion he offered on the 2d of December to negotiate with France through
the medium of an authorised minister.

About this period my communications with several of my constituents led me to think my conduct was not generally approved by them. You pressed me for explanations. I sent you Mr. Fox's letter. This did not content you. How, indeed, could it satisfy men who believed in the facility of " frowning down" mischevious opinions, who thought France would fall an easy conquest, and who were eager to become the punishers of crimes which cried aloud to heaven for vengeance? Do you now see the fallacy of these proud hopes? Do you believe that Ministers have, by their measures, gained the constitution more friends than enemies? or that they can conquer France? or change her government without conquering her? Or in one word, that you have not been made the dupes of your high-spirited sentiments, and of some of the best, as well as the worst passions of human nature? It is my turn to be importunate. I ask you whether every event that has happened since the breaking out of this war abroad, or at home, and every part of the reasoning on which in this its third year you hear ministers justifying its continuance to parliament, does not demonstrate the soundness of those opinions condemned so vehemently in those days of your phrenzy, the profound sagacity, the penetrating view, as well as the unexam-

pled fortitude of him who sacrificed his
ambition, his popularity, and hazarded
even his fame in their support?

Let us, on this subject, come to a fair
explanation. It is not one of the least
evils of your situation that you have all been
kept in profound ignorance as to what you
wished yourselves. Puzzled by your passions, you saw neither the path you were
about to quit, nor that which you meant to
pursue. Censuring me for my perseverance in opposition, what did you desire?
That I should be neutral? By no means:
I was to support somebody. But whom?
Mr. Burke, or Mr. Pitt?

You are not to imagine that this was a
matter of indifference, or capable of an
easy decision except in very easy minds. I
have already remarked to you that at the
commencement of our war system, a most
important difference of opinion subsisted
between these two persons. Mr. Burke
declared openly, and at once, for war, on
the broad ground of general policy and necessity. With larger views, a bolder imagination, and far keener feelings, he avowed his object to be no less than the restoration, by force of arms, of the French monarchy, entire, in the family of Bourbon.
The sentiments of Mr. Pitt were widely different. During the whole of this period of
consternation, while France had settled

herself in the heart of Germany, had seized Savoy, menaced Italy, and was advancing to the gates of Holland by the conquest of the Netherlands, he professed to be actuated by no other views than those of a most rigid neutrality. Far from discovering any danger to Europe from the progress of the French arms, or any insecurity for the British constitution in the establishment of a republic in France, Mr. Pitt never once offered to interfere by remonstrance, mediation, force, in short in any avowed mode whatever, until they had passed an absurd decree about the navigation of the Scheld, and put their red night caps upon the feverish heads of some of our countrymen at Paris; and then his very first step was to negociate, (as he pretends to call his interchange of memorials) with these subverters of monarchy, order, religion, and law, for the express purpose of procuring from *them* satisfactory explanations upon these, and all other matters in dispute. While Mr. Windham, Sir Gilbert Elliot, and others, stated their separation from Mr. Fox to have been because, as well upon a principle of right, as upon a balance of inconveniences, he judged the establishment of a republic in France to be a lesser evil than the destruction which he foresaw would involve Europe by an attempt to prevent it, Mr. Pitt, with whom they de-

clared an union, avowedly went in principle to every length of Mr. Fox's proposition, preferring only to conduct his negociations through agents who might be mutually disavowed. I will not accuse these
gentlemen of being influenced by any
wrong motives; but own myself anxious
to make it clear to you, that between systems so very opposite a man of plain manners might honestly doubt which he should
take part with, or whether with either. If,
for example, I had been convinced by the
reasons of Mr. Pitt, or to speak more accurately, by his concessions to his adversaries
in debate, that nothing could be so absurd
as the idea of going to war to restore the
French monarchy, and that the only dispute we had with France related to certain
wrongs she had offered us, and to points
cognizable by the law of nations, I did not
see how it was possible to resist Mr. Fox's
proposition to appeal to that law in the regular mode, by discussing, through persons
mutually authorised, the allegations of
wrong and injury under their different
heads. But if I had thought a war right
according to the principles on which Mr.
Burke and his friends argued it, then it
will follow that by giving my whole confidence and support to Mr. Pitt, I should
have put it in his power to patch up a
peace at his own convenience, and as soon

as he had carried his petty subordinate objects, without touching those larger ones,
the importance of which had persuaded me
not only of the necessity of the war, but of
its wisdom. After bending up my mind to
the risque of this perilous encounter, and
steeling my heart to all the virtuous sym-
pathies of private life, and to every sense of
pity for the wretched race of man, I should
have found the purpose for which all this
was done but very little advanced; that
another, and a yet more important question remained behind; and that I was to
say whether to accomodate a minister's
schemes, I would not give up that very
set of opinions the protection and preservation of which had been the motive to all
my sacrifices. Believing with Mr. Burke,
that the republic of France must pull down
the monarchy of England, and consequently that war was our only hope for safety,
with what consistency could I have acted
on Mr. Pitt's reasoning which left the republic untouched, or how could I have departed from opinions so dear to me as to
render the firmest friendships but lightly
valued in comparison with them, and support a war on a footing which involved
their disavowal? I saw no escape from this
dilemma. According to Mr. Burke, monarchy in Great Britain had not a day to

live after monarchy in France. According
to Mr. Pitt, it was in no danger beyond
the means which France could exert against
it, whether as a monarchy, or as a republic.

You see, Sir, that it was not well possible for men to be more adverse in principle than the members of the new alliance.
All the topics which were in use with one
branch of it, were in direct contradiction
to the professions of the other. But the
publick could not follow both. One must
give way; and to whose lot this would fall,
it was not very difficult to foresee. Mr.
Burke and his friends had made no conditions in their surrender to the minister; and
he was a man very little likely to grant
them advantages to which they were not
entitled by their situation. All this they
saw, and disregarded. Mr. Pitt, a man
with no earthly care about the French monarchy, or any monarchy, offered them
but one choice. It was war and himself,
or peace and Mr. Fox. Driven to a necessity to them so hard and afflicting, what
could they do? War, the result of their
judgments, was a bait no little tempting to
their passions. Once thoroughly involved
in war, they thought the chance of events
must bring them together upon some common principle of carrying it on. Pursuing
this view, they preferred a compromise

K

with Mr. Pitt, whose professed opinions, and whose visible interest in the destruction of the Whig party, led him to war, although on a narrow principle, to one with Mr. Fox, who with a view of putting it, if at all necessary, on a broad, national, defensive principle, proposed a measure which might have prevented it altogether.

After the issue of their experiment you will wonder no longer that, instead of appearing before you in sackcloth and ashes for the part I bore in these debates, I take to myself a sort of melancholy pride in the midst of our afflicting reverses. Never, indeed, did that general precept, so much a favourite with Mr. Burke and all wise men, that we must not begin to pull down before we have provided a plan, and materials for building up again, influence me so forcibly as during the whole of these strange proceedings. It taught me how much those members of the Whig association had to answer for, who broke up at once, and without any decent warning, that solemn compact and covenant to which they, and you, and all of us, were equally parties. Heavily will it lie on them to prove that something had crept into the party so radically, and extensively vicious, as to render of no effect all the remedies which could have been applied in the spirit of a moderating, healing compromise among our leaders. Unless they can do this, they will stand responsible to posterity to a degree the extent of which is only to be measured by those benefits and blessings they professed to transmit to it by means of their union. For what have they gained to counterbalance them? What is the end of all this hasty confidence of their's with regard to the dearest objects of their pursuit. What is the state of France? What the situation of Europe? What the condition of their own country? Painful indeed must be their feelings on a retrospect of the last three years. This improvident surrender to the will of a minister who had neither capacity, nor heart, for the situation in which he was placed, has produced the total failure of the war in all its parts. The loss of the Netherlands and Holland, the extirpation of the wretched remnant of royalists in France, the calamities which afflict, and the disgrace which humbles every part of Europe, all have their causes in this fault committed at the outset, which in some was nothing worse than an egregious blunder, but in others was the result of the grossest duplicity. Instead of laying down a clear system of war, and of alliance after war, such as we have seen pursued tolerably well from the revolution until our own days, they have helped the minister to make, and carry on a war which both in its principle and its conduct, resembles more an affray of chance medley than a national contest. In this antick garb they have suffered him to send out into the world this child of their old age to mock and disgrace their doating fancies. Such are the principles to which he has restricted the justice and necessity of a war they were so anxious for, principles so opposite to their own, that to provide the means of acting together even from day to day, they are compelled to generalize, and widen their ground, until nothing remains but the jargon about the preservation of civil society, a principle which, as a ground for war, eludes all reasoning, and in whose wide and trackless waste whatever is declared and definite in the objects of either of them, disappears, and is lost even to the speculation.

To resign small differences, and recede from the common pertinacities of opposition in times of danger, is a duty which, generally stated, I will not dispute. To have done so in a yet greater degree at the period we are considering, may possibly be very excusable in many of the instances in which it has occurred. But always, in these cases, the differences we propose to abandon must be such as we are capable of forgetting. They must be not merely such as, in a public view, we

may think ourselves warranted to suspend,
but such as we are morally certain can
never occur again. If they are to give way
at all, it must be to make room for some
plan generally good in itself, and applicable to those exigencies which shall
have necessitated, by their immediate pressure, the sacrifice, to a certain degree, of
our opinions. The opinions thus given up
must be of such a nature, as not to involve
the persons who sacrifice them in any inconsistency of principle in concerting such
a plan with those to whom the sacrifice is
offered. This never can be the case, where
the differences have gone fundamentally to
principles on which the constitution is built,
as well as to those on which government
has been administered. Then there can be
no prospective view of public advantage
in the surrender. It will go to nothing
more than an abject acknowledgment that
we have been totally mistaken in the principle of our opposition from the beginning. We cannot capitulate; we must
yield at discretion. The consequences are,
that instead of binding a minister to the
terms of a fair compromise, by thus invit-
ing him to dispose of us and our differences
just as he likes himself, he will be sure to
persist in the very same system of measures which originally made us think that
in our opposition to it we had no choice;

that the salvation of the empire depended
upon its change. He will pursue this, with
the additional mischief of receiving from
our suspension of hostilities, the means of
carrying it into the most complete effect.
This good-humoured condescension is sure,
in the first instance, to be fatal to ourselves.
It will be worse : it will be fatal to every
object we have been in the habits of connecting with our conduct and principles ;
in every hope of good example ; to every
rational purpose of unanimity itself. He
who is to reap the benefit of our submission, will study very little either our convenience or our honour, and keep barely
within the pale of not provoking us to re-
vive those sorts of disputes with him which
may tend to weaken his authority. Instead of acting together in a fair, manly
concert, the only way by which any junction can be efficacious, our time will be
spent in little partial quarrels, and re-
concilements, and soothing, and flattery, to
keep matters quiet a few days longer. In
the mean while the public cause advances
nothing ; all is left to chance ; to the un-
checked levity, and delirious presumption
of incapacity. The results are visited upon
us. Public distress, instead of shrowding,
brings out, and exposes to broad day every
shade and speck of our private disgrace ;
until at last we are delivered up, cause,

sentiments, interests, and all, to those whom we have abandoned, and thrown upon the mercy of an injured and offended friendship.

If you will take the trouble to carry these observations with you into the details of our public transactions for two years and more, you will find them correctly to describe the conduct, and possibly to anticipate the fate, of those gentlemen whose example you wished me to follow. They fell into a snare which the sober recollection of past times enabled me to avoid. To my view, the service Mr. Pitt required of them was plain and evident. He took these gentlemen along with him exactly as far as the vehement Tory spirit they shewed suited his purpose of disuniting us, and not one inch further. The war for which they were so anxious he granted them ; but in all that regarded either its principle or its management, whether as to concert with the German princes, or as the degree in which the English people were to consider themselves embarked in it, he kept his own counsel, without agreement, or consultation with them, of any kind. In many respects, even his objects were different from theirs. In one it was diametrically opposite ; for while the others were pledging themselves deeper and deeper every day not only to the war, but the war system, and cutting off every

possiblity of *their* retreat, this minister, in
the ful tempest of his indignation against
Jacobns and their adherents, had his eye
ever steadily bent towards the way by
which *his* could be kept open. Here
is in ne word, the cause of all that
perplexity, contradiction, weakness, and
want f system, which has marked the
condut of the coalesced powers. To keep
his plce at a peace, he has relaxed the
sinews f war. To keep his place at a
peace, e has unfeelingly sported with the
distress of the unfortunate emigrants.
To keo his place at a peace, he has af-
fixed te national stamp to a mass of per-
plexed unintelligible, hypocritical, and
fraudent declarations with regard to the
groune on which the war rests, equally
disgraful to the country holding out
such iidious invitations, and destructive
of all onest concert with those whom
they vre intended to conciliate. All
this, r, was mean and little. To be
actuate by such paltry predelictions was
below ie character of a great man. To
indulghim in them, was by no means the
part toe expected from a wise one. The
true frids of the war, by so doing, have
destroyl the better half of their purpose.
No soer had they delivered themselves
up to h, than they saw that the very first
use heiade of his power, was to deliver

them up to Mr. Fox. They saw, that to
secure his retreat he abandoned them on
almost every one of the points on which
they had grounded their separation from Mr.
Fox : That he conceded the question of a
republic in France, with a proviso of its
being a *good* republic ; of which *goodness*
he constituted himself the sole judge, giving them, however, no definite principle
by which they might guess at his opinions :
That he conceded the question of the personal characters of those who execute government in France. They have heard him
concede so much as to be convinced, as
every body else is, that whenever he attempts to make peace, he must act on the
principles laid down in Mr. Fox's letter to
his constituents. " Let him paint an inch
thick, to this complexion he must come at
last." He must not only negociate with
these republicans, which Mr. Burke never
would do at all, but negociate in Mr. Fox's
manner, by an authorised minister.

You know this too. You have begun to
learn it in the loss of sixty millions of your
money, and of sixty thousand lives, either
of British produce or of British purchase.
You might have read it yet more clearly in
that train of concession which ran through
almost every one of his speeches. For how
stands the question? First of all, in contra-
vention to Mr. Burke, he has admitted to Mr.

Fox, *that we need not have gone to war because France willed her present republic.*
Next he has admitted, and for this I desire no
more than the fact of his having negociated
with an unauthorized agent, *that after the ca-
tastrophe of the* 21*st of January,* 1793, *peace
might have been preserved.* Again he has admitted, that peace may *now* be made, France
remaining a republic, *and such as she is ac-
tually,* provided there be left no other subject of dispute. Lastly, he has acknowledged *that the personal characters of those
at the head of affairs, is no bar to the conclusion of a permanent treaty.* The fair
result of all these admissions is, that there
was nothing in the invasion of the Netherlands, nothing in the decree of fraternity,
nothing in the murder of Louis XVI.
nothing in the whole series of extravagan-
cies and crimes committed by the Brissots,
and the Roberspieres, by the rabble whom
they governed, or those by whom they
were guillotined, of force sufficient to prevent our receiving both satisfaction, indemnification, and security, for us, and the
rest of Europe, provided these persons for
the sake, or on the speculation of keeping
their power, had only been wise enough to
give it us in sufficient quantity. These
were the objects publicly held forth to the
world, objects so distinct from those of
Mr. Burke, that nothing but a private

understanding between the parties, that there should be war at any rate, could have kept up for one moment the semblance of co-operation between them. But Mr. Pitt thought he had done enough for these gentlemen in giving them the war they were so eager for, without shutting himself out from the prospect of making peace whenever the country should grow tired of it; and this he was cunning enough to know was only to be done by declaring war under such reserves and limitations as those which Mr. Fox appeared to extort from him during the debates.

Such were his concessions. Such is the line of separation he marked out, very early in the contest, between himself and his new friends. With his purpose in so doing, all his public declarations most accurately correspond. There are two senses in all of them. As it has been said of him by a very close observer of human nature, *whenever he speaks to you he places a substantive between two adjectives of an opposite meaning.* The war has not made him forget this, his favourite part of speech. Having determined upon it, to gain the seceders from the Whig party, and upon assigning reasons which should enable him to get out of it whenever he liked, it became his policy to perplex and entangle as much as possible, the threads of this mystic skein in which he

held so many of our tender consciences fast
bound and locked up. Accordingly he
stated, as you may remember, that the
points at issue with France were reducible
to the three following---to REPARATION
for an unprovoked aggression, INDEMNI-
FICATION for our expences in seeking it,
and SECURITY against future attempts.
With regard to the two first, there was very
little room for introducing into the discussions concerning them any perplexity in the
least propitious to his wishes. Even those
who carried highest their opinions in favour of the monarchy, never disputed the
full practical competency of Roberspierre,
or any you will name, to satisfy us. Putting
the justice of our claim for a moment out
of the question, it must be owned that
France had not much to repair, or to indemnify us for, in the month of February
1793, and to whatever extent we since have
conceived ourselves entitled to ask for indemnification, the modes of it could equally be settled by the present, or by any set
of rulers that France, in her folly, might
give herself. If money was to indemnify
us, doubtless we should not have scorned
to receive, even from the hands of Roberspierre, the gold he had plundered from the
church. To the reproaches of Mr. Burke,
the minister probably would have answered
in the words of a Roman emperor, whose

chancellor of the exchequer was not, it
should seem, over delicate in the choice of
his ways and means. * If territory was
to be the mode, we doubtless should have
been as ready then, as I take it we are now,
to accept St. Domingo under a treaty with
the Convention, as we were to enter Toulon
under a capitulation with the French royalists. These two points, therefore, of reparation and indemnification were easily
disposed of. The great question was the
security. Here was a subject of chicane
without end. Here was a field for the display of all those ambidextrous contrivances, of all those tricks and shuffles so easy
to the imagination under no restraint from
principle. On this it was that he played
double during the whole of that session, as
he has ever since, alternately resorting to
the systems of Mr. Burke and Mr. Fox, according to the degree in which they bore
on that first object of his cares, the preservation of his office and the disjunction of
his opponents.

To keep the game entirely within his
own hands, he cautiously avoided all explanation of the term " Security," even as
he understood it himself. Whenever the
war was mentioned incidentally, in the
House, he enforced the triple ground on

* *Reprehendenti Tito pecuniam admovit ad nares, scîscitans num
odore offenderetur? et illo negante,* ATQUI, *inquit* E LOTIO EST.
Suet.

which he had put it by a set of arguments which had an effect, as by him it
was intended that they should, far beyond
the immediate question he was debating,
and which, as well as puzzling the question of Security, gave him the additional
advantage of confounding it with that of
Indemnity. Declarations to this import
were frequently repeated during the first
sessions of the war. If no two men understood him the same way, it was enough
for his purpose that every friend to the
war understood him in his own. It seemed,
however, that the further we advanced in
the business of this war, the darker and
the more slippery became our way. On
the 28th of August Lord Hood and Don
Juan Langara entered the port of Toulon.
They took possession of it, and of the ships
at anchor there, under *a treaty* with the
inhabitants of the place, to hold them *in
trust for Lewis XVII.* whom they acknowledged as *King of the French, under
the Constitution of* 1791. As in this treaty
not a syllable was said about reparation, indemnification, or security, while the French
nation on the other hand was invited to
repair to the standard erected at Toulon
for the monarchical constitution of 1791,
Mr. Pitt found himself under the necessity
of counteracting an opinion which then
began to prevail, and which was so far

dangerous to his views as it pledged him
against any terms with any sort of republic. Accordingly, on the 23d of Octo-
ber, a declaration, or manifesto, is put
forth, addressed to all the foreign ministers, and to all commanders of his Majesty's fleets and armies, and more particularly to the French nation. Always
ready as I am to pay the profoundest homage to his talents when I see them em-
ployed on these exercises of ingenuity, to
do them full justice on this occasion can
be the work of no hands but his own. To
this most extraordinary paper I shall beg
a few moments of your attention. Its
character is in its matter. It admits of no
close description, since it is the index of
the mind of him who put it together. In
this performance it must be confessed,
that no part of his various excellencies is
hid by the envious interception of intelligence, or principle of any kind. It seems
to have been imagined in the idea of conciliating all parties to the war, by exhibiting, in a piece which should contain a little
of every body's, a specimen of that amiable
unanimity which prevailed among the ministers themselves. It was contrived to
look like a joint effort of cabinet ingenuity,
to which every member contributed his
separate portion of wisdom, which he took
care so to distinguish from his neighbour's

as to be sure of no difficulty in making out
his claim to it hereafter. It was an assem-
blage in which monarchies, republics, war,
peace, religion, atheism, dire bloodshed, and
halcyon harmony, mingled together in a
groupe wholly new and fanciful; forming a
sort of *divertissement* somewhat between a
Pyrrhick dance and a Scotch reel; a whimsi-
cal fairy fandango, which presented in its
turn to the eye every variety of shape and
attitude; but which, when you approached
to join hands with it, vanished into the
thin air of which it was composed. With
all this, the deception was admirable. Every
man looked at it in his own way, and became satisfied with the resemblance he
found to his own notions. Nothing was
ever hit off in such rare felicity of mischief. He had framed a declaration which,
it is true, did not directly disavow Lord
Hood : that were to have spoken too
plainly in another sense : but although
not an actual, it was one that might be
understood as a virtual disavowal; or, if
that would not do, as tantamount to a virtual disavowal. If there yet remained any
persons---still determined, in spite of the
constant ambiguity of his language, to trust
to his management---who fancied that they
could pick out, from the operations of the
war, a distinct object which prudential reasons induced him to keep back, and who,

under this impression, had embarked in the cause of monarchy with zeal and spirit, in the belief that in so doing they were committing themselves to his views no further than as he was assisting them in theirs; here they found at once the short and certain end to whatever had appeared clear and hopeful to them in these prospects. The text had been revised afresh. The original doubtful reading was restored. Reparation, Indemnification, and Security, those words of potent spell, regained their credit, somewhat weakened, it must be owned, by the preference recently shewn to that of Monarchy at Toulon. The sentiments of those who agreed to the war in his view of it, but objected to one the professed purpose of which was to settle the disturbances of France, and of those who, like Mr. Burke, deemed nothing else worth contending about, were here blended together, and made to harmonize in a composition impoverished by no œconomy of fraud, confined to no single order of duplicity, but lavishly displaying the whole resources of the art worked up into a master-piece by a master-hand. To the first description of persons he addresses himself in language such as this—" His " Majesty by no means disputes the *Right* " of France to reform its laws. It never " would have been his wish to employ the

M

" influence of external force with respect
" to the particular forms of government to
" be established in an independent coun-
" try." To these he holds up his two
points of indemnity, and security, as standing by themselves; totally disconnected from
the question of her government, and rendered important and indispensable *only* on
the ground of the progress of the arms of
France, and her forcible seizure of the territories of other powers. This view of the
subject he sustains by the chain of reasoning we have before had occasion to advert
to in considering the nature of his concessions, and which is applicable to no other.
But when he speaks to the next set of supporters, a very different language is adopted.
Another ingredient must be thrown into
the cauldron to bind the charm. The king
is then made to " *demand*" from France,
" some legitimate and stable government,
" founded on the acknowledged principles
" of universal justice, and capable of main-
" taining with other powers the accustomed
" relations of peace and amity." From this
government the king would exact " none
" other than equitable and moderate con-
" ditions; *not such* as the expences, the
" risques, and the sacrifices of the war
" might justify; but such as his majesty
" thinks himself under the indispensable ne-
" cessity of requiring with a view to those
" considerations," &c. &c. Here the plot

thickens!---indemnity is confounded with security, and security with the question of government, from which before it had been kept distinct. Here the security is made to depend not upon the cession of towns, fortresses, or provinces to any number or extent, which in the other view of the subject might constitute a satisfactory one, but upon the adoption on the part of France of what we, not they, may happen to think a " legitimate" government. Who embarrasses the security with this condition? The king of Great Britain, who had just before declared that he " *by no means disputes* " *with France, the right to reform its* " *laws.*" The king of Great Britain, who can't bear to think of employing " *the in-* " *fluence of external force with respect to* " *the particular forms of government to* " *be established in an independent country.*" This you acknowledge to be inconsistent. I wish it were nothing worse. It might then be neutral in the scale of evil. But what name shall we find for the inconsistency that springs from Will and is accompanied with Power? In any other case, it would be the caprice of an odious despotism. All however was acquiesced in that Mr. Pitt might be enabled to secure himself by talking the language of monarchy to Mr. Burke, and that of money and profit on the royal exchange.

If I had been ever so much disposed to concur in Mr. Burke's general view of the wisdom of a war with France, I certainly should not have carried my complaisance to the minister so far, as to take, in return for all the sacrifices that concurrence would have required, a war upon such terms. If right at all, it was right upon Mr. Burke's principles, which, as well as being the only ones to defend it by, were those which led to the only means that gave a chance for its successful termination. On these principles it should have been declared, not waited for. Least of all should it have been waited for as Mr. Pitt affected to do, daily provoking the formal declaration of it on the part of France, by acts which were in truth and substance, a declaration of it on his own. In all this to be sure there was risque; as where is the situation without it? There was the risque of his place first, in the supposition that the country would not go with him in a war so declared. There was a second risque, in the event itself; since, after declaring war on such a principle, there was no *mode* of a republic with which he could treat. But is it true that we are a country so lost, that we are in a condition so abandoned of virtue and heaven, as to see no resource beyond the existence of a minister, whose only talent is the dexterity with which he avoids the adoption of

any decisive course in the season of public
· extremity? Sir, these habits may suit little
affairs, and the moment of profound peace,
in which a country like ours may be said
almost to govern itself; but I know of no
severer curse it can labour under than the
rule of such a minister, who when the
storm is up, and danger affronts us on every
side, can look to no object firmly, or without glancing aside to his own place. In
vain do we share his risques: In vain do
we wake and watch, and urge him with
every argument, and tempt him with every
sacrifice. Weakness and irresolution meet
us at every corner; the cause is betrayed;
and those who conscientiously support him
in it are made the scape-goats of his miserable ambition.

They who reason closely upon the nature of Mr. Pitt's admissions at the outset
of this business, will surely see the mistake in which they have suffered their
passions to hurry them by jumping in
with his conclusions to the justice and
necessity of a war. On the principles
avowed by Mr. Burke and his friends, it
is at least easy to understand by what chain
of argument, and through what deductions
of expediency, they make it out. They
put their objections to Mr. Fox's proposal
for negociating with France upon its true
ground. They argued, that the sending,
or receiving an authorised minister, would

imply a recognition of the French republic; that by such an act we should dispirit,
and wholly destroy, the royal cause; that
it was unwise, at a moment in which we
had been *forced by the principles of France*,
into a war with her, to begin the conflict
by a measure which would leave her no
care for the security of her power at home,
whereas by an opposite course she would
set out in her foreign contest, with a fierce
civil war in the very heart of her territory.
In Mr. Burke's view, this doctrine was assuredly correct, and if the reasoning on
which it was founded had been followed up
to its true point, I am ready to confess that
whatever might have been my other objections to the war, those which belonged
to the deceitful indistinctness of its principle whould have been entirely done away,
and that which was grounded upon the im-
practicability of recovering the monarchy
very much diminished. But how ought
this reasoning to have been followed up?
By a direct declaration on our parts in favour of the infant monarch; by a national
recognition of his title; by connecting that
title, and the principles on which it was
claimed for him, with those enlarged principles in relation to civil society and social
order now foisted into every silly harangue
which begs us to trust the minister whether
he disposes himself to war for the monarchy,

or to peace with the republic. It should have been followed up, not by cold, occasional exhortations to choose, but by active co-operation to restore, a monarch; and by setting up, and exhibiting under the sanction of the British nation, the descendant of so many kings in an adverse point of view to a republic founded on so many crimes. We ought to have shewn the faithful description of persons yet attached to the monarchy that the nations of Europe interested themselves in their cause for the cause itself; that a sense of their own safety *as connected with the re-establishment of monarchy in France,* had dictated the terms of a general confederacy for its restoration; that all ancient animosities were laid aside, as well as all those views of ambition and aggrandizement among each other which had kept those animosities alive; and that as a proof of their sincerity towards France, and as it were to be a guard over, and a security against, themselves, they had placed at their head a nation long renowned for integrity and plain dealing, itself enjoying a just government by law, under whose preponderating influence all the operations of the war, and all the arrangements to be made for the cure of their miseries, would be directed.

It was by such a declaration alone that our cause as against the government of

France, could derive any effectual aid.
The point which, in this whole contest,
seems the least to admit of any dispute, is
that the co-operation of a royalist force in
the interior of France was essential to your
other exertions. But without some such
declaration as that which I have alluded
to, I think you ought not to have claimed
that co-operation, and that you could not
have obtained it. It has been argued indeed, that ministers would have been very
much embarassed by such a step. That
the royal cause had many supporters of opposite and adverse ways of thinking; that
it was impossible to declare for one set,
without offending and alienating the other,
and that it was better to act as they did
with a view to unite, as well every description of royalists, as all other persons who
might wish to withdraw themselves from
the tyranny of the convention. Those who
offer this apology for ministers are compelled to maintain that they must either have
said absolutely nothing at all on the subject
of monarchy, or have held out, as they
did, all sorts of hopes to all sorts of royalists, since it was only in these two ways
that they could secure the object which
they thought so wise, of avoiding all dis-
tinctness and specification. The first answer I should make to this, would be from
the fact of their conduct at Toulon. I

know it is said that Lord Hood pledged
this country to nothing there beyond hcre-
ditary monarchy. The treaty says the reverse; and that the sort of monarchy then
stipulated for was hereditary monarchy,
*with certain limitations expressed and spe-
cified by a law of their own making.* Of
those limitations there were probably many
which the good sense of the French nation
would have rejected or altered, when they
came to the final settlement of their constitution; but it is not in common reason to
suppose that they would have given up
that in which was to consist the whole difference between the government they were
endeavouring to establish, and that which
they had just destroyed. Shall it therefore
be argued that Lord Hood engaged for
nothing but the old monarchy, when by
the mere mention of that of 1789 he recognized in the name of his master, who
never disavowed him, the legitimacy of it's
subversion? admit this to me, which you
must, and I must argue that the treaty was
valid as between Lord Hood, representing
the King of Great Britain, and the Tou-
lonese virtually taken to represent the royalists in France, *quoad* the principle of
these limitations; that the sort of royalism
in the contemplation of his Majesty's Ministers here was the royalism specified by the
first revolution in 1789; and that by autho-
N

rizing Lord Hood so to do, they acted not only in direct opposition to their own declared principle of avoiding all specification, but acted most unwisely by declaring in favour of that particular specification which was sure of placing an eternal bar between them and any of the old royalists who were then exerting themselves in la Vendée. Unless, however, the " common cause" of the allies was such as the genuine Royalists of France could not honourably co-operate with, I affirm that this affected avoidance of all specification was the worst judged piece of political prudery ever imagined. Ministers were not by any means reduced to a dilemma between these two descriptions of persons; nor was it required of them to make any specification of the nature of that which was hazarded at Toulon. All that they were called upon to do, was to declare for monarchy, and for hereditary monarchy, in the person of Louis XVII. accompanied, undoubtedly, in the view in which I am now considering the subject, with an engagement from the whole confederacy *not to make peace or truce with France until these points should be obtained.* To come to some definite understanding on this subject was absolutely necessary; as much so was it to communicate the decision to the royal party, become ONE as it must have been by a candid proceeding of the allies, both in, and out of France. Those unhappy men would then have had an opportunity of knowing on what terms they were to act: Whether it would be most adviseable to agree, possibly, to the dismemberment of their country for the sake of living under a monarch in the part which should remain to it, or whether to submit to the revolution, and take their chance for better times.

Could it, for instance, be reasonable to exclude, from *any* project of carrying on this war against France, a party which at the period I speak of is not to be undervalued by counting it at any given number of men, but which then could only be estimated by a description comprising the extent of the territory they occupied, the whole of whose vast population started up in arms at the voice of their chiefs? Some sort of intercourse and concert, all admit, should have been kept up with them. What intercourse? What concert? I answer that which should take for its foundation an honest declaration in favour of monarchy, and which, wisely leaving all its limitations to be settled by Frenchmen alone, should confine itself to proving the sincerity of the confederates by a pledge in the nature of that to which I have alluded.

But this, after all, was a wild and chimerical project. So be it. I promise you

that I shall have nothing to object to the
arguments of those who maintain that we
never ought to have mixed in these troubles. My only business with the question
is in its comparative view with Mr. Pitt's
principle; to which I prefer Mr. Burke's
all to nothing. For let me put it to your
common sense, whether a system could
have been pursued more in unison with
jacobinism itself, than the whole of that on
which the minister has conducted this
war? Was there ever a man before him
who engaging in a war any part of the object of which was the rescuing a country
from the miseries of anarchy, neglected to
hold out distinctly to it any sort of inducement founded upon the state of things intended to be set up in lieu of that anarchy?
How many royalists has this foolish cunning banished into hopeless inactivity?
How many republicans have we roused to
the field, who would have been content to
smile at the sword and the manifestoes of
the Duke of Brunswick? For again let me
ask, what sense was there at any time in
refusing to treat with the French republic?
Assuredly none—if it was for the indul-
gence of an idle punctilio; but the case
is somewhat different when the refusal is
put upon the ground of giving heart to
those within France with whom the great
measures of the war would have been con-

certed by wise ministers. It would have been right to attack France with the weapons peculiar to such a war. For one, I should have speculated for success upon the joint co-operating force of external war, and internal insurrection. In this point of view, I can understand the resistance made to Mr. Fox's motion; because there is certainly some sense in making the refusal to treat a *cause* of war, when you make it also a powerful *instrument* for carrying it on. But to take this line with any hope of success, the most indispensable of all things was good faith, and a perfect intelligence on all points with the people I was to act with. I am not going to descant in common places upon the necessity of good faith; but look to the peculiar species of war in which our fortune has engaged us, . and then tell me whether the system pursued by ministers has not been fatal to every one of their objects, chiefly on the grounds of its ill faith? You know to what a degree the old royalists of France detest the constitutionalists of 1789. They have not one sentiment or feeling in common with each other even in the midst of their common distresses. His Majesty's ministers, however, told you that it was a great point with them to get the aid of these two parties against the existing French government; and that therefore it was expedient to carry on an understanding with each. Now let me ask, whether it be possible that where parties have no common object arising from opinion, a third can mediate between them without betraying both? He that puts himself in that situation begins by holding a language to entrap the confidence of each, which instead of using to any of the fair purposes for which it is entrusted to him, he carries to market upon a principle of mere profit and loss, and sells the one to the other, or both to a better bidder, just as a bargain may happen to suit him. All he is anxious to avoid is the giving to either of these parties a particular title to reproach him. Under the cover of this stupid insincerity he huggs himself in the prospect of being able to deal out impartial treachery to all sides. Weak policy, this, as applied to any situation; but contemptible beyond all imagination when applied to our intercourse with the French royalists. Never was plain dealing so necessary: never was honour so little to be separated from wisdom, as in all our transactions with that unfortunate set of men. In common affairs we may sometimes venture to go great lengths, with a view to some act of manifest public benefit, with those whom we may know to be deceiving us. Great nations, hating each other in their hearts, may yet be brought to act to-

gether in a well regulated confederacy.
No man is deceived by the language of
treaties, much less the courts themselves with
which they happen to be negociated. The
security of independent European nations,
generally speaking, lies in this, that in the
present situation of the world, if one Ally
fail them, they are, upon the whole, tolerably sure of supplying his place with another. But widely different is the case when
you are to form an union with a party in a
country against its government. They in
France who are to call you friends, trust
you with their all. If you are to enter into
engagements with such persons they should
be solemn, and binding upon you in proportion to the awful magnitude of the trust
you undertake. You cannot engage them
to run the risque of so perilous a correspondence, in a country where the least of their
dangers is the mighty force they will have
to contend against, without subjecting yourselves to a moral responsibility far greater
than any that I am capable of imagining.
What, Sir, should I be able to say to those
deluded men who had escaped from im-
prisonment, torture, famine, and the sword,
who, cherishing their loyalty in the midst
of a thousand hardships, had consented to
crawl about their wretched country in all
the bitterness of woe, exposed to every species of anguish that can afflict, or want

that can debase the mind, in the fond hope, taught them by your promise, that we should come to restore them to their honours and estates, when we present to their parched lips the dregs of their cup of sorrow, and bid them swallow down the constitution of 1789? Or what face could I shew to the Royalist of 1789, who, on the plighted faith of the British government, had taken arms against the Convention and helped to pull down its power, when for the reward of his services and his risques, I should deliver him up to be punished as a traitor by the ministers of the old despotism which he had helped to re-establish? I put it to you, Sir, as a zealous well-wisher to the cause of French monarchy, whether the recognition of the Republic on Mr. Fox's principles would not have been ten thousand times more eligible, and even a shorter way to its restoration, than these insidious contrivances to hook in the various parties in France by appearing all things to all men, while in fact we pledged ourselves honestly to nothing.

I am indeed infinitely more inclined to ascribe our failure to this double dealing in ministers, than to any superiority of military prowess, or conduct, in the French armies. There was a moment,—it was in the first campaign, about the period of the surrender of Valenciennes, and the re-capture of Mayence, followed by the forcing the passage into Alsace by the allies, when the destruction of the republic seemed almost within the reach of men who knew how to make use of their advantages. Royalism then triumphed in La Vendeé,—federalism in Normandy and in Gascony,—insurrection at Toulon, Marseilles, and Lyons,---the frontiers were abandoned or forced---famine was at Paris---fear was every where. This was the decisive moment in which a little sincerity might have given you France. Why was it missed? In two words I will answer---because neither sincerity nor capacity belonged to Administration; because, for purposes of their own, they had put this war on a footing which forbade all honest co-operation between the allies, and those within the territories of France with whom a common object could have been concerted. The reason is to be found in that spirit of faithless indecision between the two schemes of dismemberment and monarchy; schemes for ever floating before their eyes, and tempting them with the prospect of advantages between which they knew not how to choose. They have failed, not for want of the resources common to all ministers, or of the means of persuading the country to support them, not through any impediments thrown in their way by the influence of their

O

opponents, but through the total absence of that in which true greatness consists, the ability to discern, and the vigour to determine, the preference due to different degrees of political good.

Viewing this question as a royalist, therefore, I confess I can see nothing to justify the sacrifice with which the minister was complimented by Mr. Burke and Mr. Windham. To the success of the war that sacrifice, perhaps, has been fatal. Persuaded as these gentlemen had been for a long time before, of the wisdom of a war with France, they would have done well to consider the effect upon the public mind of acceding to principles which, in order to accommodate a minister, gave up the strongest part of their question, and suffered it to go to the country upon the single argument of its necessity; a footing always doubtful, and which Mr. Pitt, as slippery an ally as he is an unfair enemy, rendered less and less tenable for them every day by those concessions I have already enumerated to you. These were my reasons Sir, for preferring, when the war questions began to be agitated, the plain strait forward road pointed out by Mr. Fox in the outset of our difficulties. I thought this the only way to relieve me from the certain inconsistency of voting for war on the principles of Mr. Pitt, or of speculating towards peace with *any* republic, after having consented to act on those of Mr. Burke. It was thus only that I could be spared the toil of chacing through the mysterious vicissitudes of principle which the war assumed every day, any one definite, or intelligible object. Standing at that distance out of the fog, it was plain to me that the contrivers of all these manœuvres were entangling themselves with their own tackle; and that between rash zeal, which promised all, and wary duplicity which was providing for its own safety, the monarchy they both professed so highly to value, as well as all those interests connected with it, would be lost sight of altogether. It was evident that the war would be crippled from the want of heart in those who claimed to be trusted with its conduct. Necessity therefore, must have ranged me on the side of Mr. Fox's proposition even if I had felt no inducement from reason and reflection to join with it. Between Mr. Burke and Mr. Pitt, I was not allowed to choose, although between the objects, and the plans of these two persons, there was every species of difference on which choice could be exercised. Our warm zealots preferred any sort of war, no matter how conducted, to what they thought the hazards of peace. For myself, retaining to the full as much disgust for the cruelties of the French as they did, and departing in no point from my old Whig opinions respecting the aggrandisement of that nation, I thought the peace ought not to have been broken for the sake of a war professedly of chances. Chance, you will say, decides much in all wars; but to leave as little to chance as possible in what we undertake, I have ever thought to be the peculiar office of prudence. We read of wars well planned and ably conducted, ending, nevertheless, very wide from their original design; but a war begun without an object, a war that was to pick up an object in its way, was reserved for the politics of this enlightened age! A war of this description, among other reflections, is sure to strike an enquiring mind very forcibly with doubts whether it might not have been avoided altogether. You begin to understand this now. You will understand it much better whenever you think seriously of peace.

For what is it that you desire of France? If this question comes too close, I take it you will allow me to answer for you that you would be glad to see in that country a king. This is your fancy: you are at no pains to disguise it. You swallow with credulous avidity all that is told you in the public prints of armies of royalists, and feed fat the ancient grudge you bear this revolution with the hopes of a famine at Paris. You, who perpetually object the instability of all government in France to our proposal for treating with her, wait with an impatience that makes sad work with your argument, for the insurrection which is to produce a king there. With him, or his ministers, or a regent in his name, you are ready to negociate. What? before a second messenger can come to tell you whether another revolution has not sent him back from his throne to his prison? Before you know whether they have *elected* for their king the descendant of a Bourbon, or the spawn of a fishwoman? Oh no! It must be the son, or since he is no more, a brother, of Louis XVI. Then it is not a king you ask of France for the sake of the office of king, but a king with limitation to a particular stock; and if you cannot be indulged in this, the war must go on. But I grant another Bourbon placed on the throne of his ancestors. What next? You can never think of treating with him until you know his ability to keep his engagements. Here is one more remove from precision in your object. What is meant by ability to keep his engagements? Who are to judge of it? Yourselves. By what rule? Not to quarrel with you for a word, I will call it by your discretion. France restores monarchy, we will say, un-

der certain limitations. You don't approve
of these limitations, or you think the monarchy not likely to be safe under them.
Consistently with your principles therefore,
you can make peace with the monarch as
little as you can with the present republic.
France must submit to you the whole
question of her government, both as to form,
to persons, and to limitations. The case
is full of all manner of embarrassments.
What will any monarchy be worth in
France unless the emigrants recover their
estates? Of the two, a demand to reinstate
them would be far the more reasonable and
the more just. These were your difficulties from the beginning; they are still the
same, and must continue so in the most
favourable turn the contest can take. They
impose on you the necessity of setting up
in France a king of your own, and of supporting him when he is there. I think it
clear, upon the face of such terms, that a
war to enforce them could not be necessary; wise, honourable, expedient, for the
present as much as you please, but that
character which is understood by the term
necessary, that is, *inevitable*, can never belong to it upon any reasoning we have yet
heard. It may fairly be thrown on the
other side therefore, to support the negative of this proposition, That no political situation in which Great Britain can be

said to have stood in the month of January 1793, made it necessary that the peace should be broken at that moment in order to hunt for a cause of quarrel so large as that which is now explained by the demand of " *a government capable of maintaining with other nations, the accustomed relations of peace and amity.*"

Here, Sir, I must stop for a few moments to notice the flimsy conceit, it deserves no better name, of those who rest the question of *necessity* on the accidental, formal declaration of war first at Paris : to such it is more than enough to answer that the insulting dismission of M. Chauvelin was the substantial declaration of it. In the strictness of public law, the notification to him not to appear at Court was giving France a just *cause of complaint* against us, which, if not settled by negociation, might become a just *cause of war.* But the dismission was an act of positive and final hostility. It was going one step farther than any act of military aggression, on which nations are apt enough to take fire, as it happened to us in a recent dispute with Spain ; because, after such an act, intercourse still remains to explain the circumstances ; but the dismission of a minister in the midst of a negociation includes both acts, that of aggression in the first place, and the refusal to explain it in the next. On this ground therefore, they who justify the war can make no impression. They must have recourse to the argument that M. Chauvelin was not a regular minister. Why was he not? They answer, because France had no regular government. I ask no more; for then I say they give up the whole argument of the necessity of the war as far as it depends upon its mere formal declaration at Paris, and must come back to the ground of social order, and so forth, which Mr. Pitt has uniformly disclaimed as having any reference to the *origin* of the war, and which therefore by a necessary and inevitable conclusion, must have been picked up in the course of it.

To return to your demands on France. The same reasoning which goes to the necessity of your fixing for France the principle of her monarchy, should she be disposed to return to it, will apply to the case of a republic, if at last you hear of one with which you incline to beat a parley. The mode in which that republic is constructed, the degree of its dependence on the body of the people, the extent of its powers executive and legislative,---all these great features must regularly pass you in revision if your principle be kept to, of not negociating but with a stable government. You cannot trust France to make it such. You must do it yourselves. As little can you trust yourselves to a republic of the Champ de Mars, as to a monarchy dug out of the common shores of the fauxbourg St. Marceau. Reserving thus to yourselves to judge what sort of government, and what only, will content you, and investing the ministers with a power to pronounce sentence upon it in your name, the object of the war is not concealed by their prudence, but called to its very existence by their will. Coming from this source, it varies according to that will, and according to every circumstance whether of public import, or of private convenience and interest, by which that will is determined. You give them thus a perpetual negative on all the modes by which France may endeavour to free herself from the calamities of her bad government. Where is the difference between this power of negative *ad infinitum* and the direct positive power of origination? This large discretion I will not now dispute may be fit and wise to lodge in the king's ministers; but where I ask are those great public interests, or that national credit and honour, the risque or the violation of which, places a government under the necessity of resorting to the dire extremity of war?

P

Every way in which you try the question, it presents you with the same results. Reverse it; and say, to the exclusion of all foreign interference, that you are ready to negociate with France, whenever she has got what you would call a fit and proper government. You must admit a capacity in France to create out of her own materials, this fit and proper government. Admitting this capacity now, you must admit that it existed always: otherwise you will puzzle yourselves with a question yet more difficult to settle than any of which this contest has been so fruitful, and that is,---When did they acquire the capacity? It is in proof against the ministers, that they " *do not dispute the right* " *of France to reform its laws :*" that they never wished to advise his Majesty " *to em-* " *ploy the influence of external force with* " *respect to the particular form of govern-* " *ment to be established in an independent* " *country.*" Thus far agreed, the question occurs—did France ever attempt to exercise this never disputed RIGHT, and to avail herself of this admitted CAPACITY? I answer, she did. France, when in September 1792, she chose the Convention which is now sitting, spoke her will plainly and distinctly; as distinctly, to say nothing more, as you can expect to hear her pronounce it under any invitation of yours.

What follows? You acknowledge her capacity; you never meant, as you say, to
dispute her will; why then did this war
commence. Under what pretext did you
refuse to receive M. Chauvelin as an au-
thorized minister? Under what pretext did
you dispute the powers by which he acted?
Under what pretext was that act of unprovoked aggression and insult, an act which
all writers on the law of nations confider as
tantamount to a declaration of war, committed against France, namely, that of or-
dering M. Chauvelin to quit the kingdom?
Was your choice free to act in this manner,
or was it not? If you could choose, you
was under no necessity, moral or physical,
of embarking in the war at the time you
did, and consequently it is fair to argue
that it might have been avoided altogether.

So much Sir, for the justice, and necessity of the sort of war which Mr. Pitt has
provided for us. I have said you would
understand better at a peace, why it might
have been avoided. I think so, because it
is then, and possibly not until then, that
you will be made thoroughly sensible of
your disgrace. Ministers seem to think
indeed, that disgrace like crime, may be
diminished by participation; and consequently, by a perverse analogy to a false
principle, that they may be acquitted of
failing in any one object of their war if they

have but the good fortune to fail in all.
I doubt their escaping so easily. Because,
whether France shall elect a monarch, or a
magistracy, if she does it of herself, if her
will prevail over your power, it comes to
the same point. Your defeat is plain and
legible. You can no more disguise it than
the simpleton can hide himself by covering his eyes with his hands. It is at the
peace that you will find, that your hostility will have been the pure loss of just so
many lives, and so many millions, and all
your honour, unless the form of government France shall set up, and which you
recognize at last, bear some unequivocal
mark of your hand, and of your having
produced it by your interposition. Even
monarchy, the daily object of your prayers,
will help you nothing. In fair truth, where
is the difference between a republic of M.
Tallien and the Abbé Seyes, and a monarchy coming out of their hands? Call it
by what name you please, it is still M.
Tallien, and the Abbé Seyes. Formed in
utter contempt of you, wanting in all it's
parts, the seal of your authority to attest
it's genuiness, be the constitution of France
monarchy, aristocracy, simple democracy,
or a confederation of republics, neither your
pride nor your convenience will be considered in the settlement.

Before, however, I dismiss the point of
necessity, I feel it incumbent upon me to

state some observations of a more general nature, in which, perhaps, I may have the good fortune to approach considerably nearer to your sentiments. It is asked, had France in January 93, given us no cause for offence or dissatisfaction? Was neutrality the right policy for us to follow while she was seizing province after province, and proclaiming common cause with disaffection and rebellion in all countries? Against this mode of stating the question, I must ever protest. It supposes that we, who contend against the principle on which the war was rested by administration, must have prepared our minds for the entire conquest of Europe by France as a matter of perfect indifference: that we had consented to abandon the ancient foreign system pursued by this country with little exception since the revolution, to limit our views to our own island, and leave the continent to take care of itself. Sir, it will ever form one of my very heaviest grounds of complaint against the administration of that time, and not less so against many of our former associates that, holding as I do, opinions the exact reverse of these, they made it impossible for me to act upon them. With every disposition to curb France, and even to assist them in an endeavour to curb her, I felt that they were determined, for unworthy party purposes, to encumber my as-

sent to the measures necessary for it,
with subscriptions to new doctrines, unknown to our fathers, and utterly inconsistent with all sound wisdom, or right principle. They rejected with disdain all offer
of support which did not leave the whole of
the war, whether with regard to it's object,
it's conduct, or it's principle, to their arbitrary caprice. In a spirit of unfair dealing
which I did not think was in their natures,
Mr. Windham, and others, countenanced a
clamour which just then began to be raised
against Mr. Fox, as if he had seen with satisfaction the progress of France in the Netherlands, and towards Germany. They
countenanced these calumnies, knowing
them to be such, knowing from long habits of consultation with him, that his whole
foreign system was framed upon a directly
opposite view, and from private explanation as well as public avowal, that his sentiments on this point continued unaltered.
These gentlemen rejected his support, because it did not go to a war without first separating the principle on which the country
was to engage in it, from that contained in
the Duke of Brunswick's manifesto. The
ministers rejected it because they knew that
if the war should stand upon any fair national principle which Mr. Fox could approve, the country would call for him to
conduct it. It seemed to be the mutual

wish of these parties to draw a line which
should separate him from all that was decent, orderly, and settled in political principle; and to drive him to seek his safety
in associating himself and his cause, with
the leaders of the English revolutionary
societies. Frightened at the proceedings
of men who wanted, as they said, nothing
but a leader to be in a capacity to pull down
King, Lords, and Commons at their pleasure, all was done, in the true character
of panick such as theirs, to make them a
present of such a leader as Mr. Fox, by
passing, as it were, a sentence of outlawry
upon him, and shutting him out from all
communion with the constitution. If personal provocation could have weighed against
a sense of duty, enough in all conscience was
offered Mr. Fox, to make him the veriest
Jacobin that ever lived. That he did not
become so, those friends of his, who, " like
the poor Judean, cast a pearl away richer
than all their tribe," may thank his honour
and consistency rather more than their own
judgment or moderation. Suffering with
him in the same cause, and guided by his
example, I declared then, and am still of
opinion, that France by her invasion of
Savoy and the Netherlands, did give to
Great Britain just grounds for offence:
that these just grounds for offence, if not
removed by negociation, would give us a

just, and a necessary ground for war. Pursuing this principle as far as it honestly
went, I did condemn the minister for not
having interfered much earlier. In my
view of the subject many occasions had
occured for this interference. First, when
the convention between the Emperor and
the King of Prussia at Pillnitz was notified
to the other powers of Europe; secondly,
when upon the breaking out of hostilities,
France threatened an invasion of the Austrian Netherlands; again, when in June,
1792, France directly applied to Great
Britain for her good offices; and again,
when the victory of Jemappe had cleared
her frontiers, and put the Austrians out of
condition to renew offensive operations. I
thought it highly criminal in the minister
not to have spoken out, at each of these
periods, in a language dictated by the spirit
of a sincere, but efficient neutrality, as well
to France as to the confederates. This it
was his duty to have done, even though his
dear place were the forfeit, instead of play-
ing off the petty artillery of intrigues at
home to set old friends at variance, and to
conciliate through the fears of some of us
a support he never could win from our ap-
probation. To every part of that ancient
system of our foreign policy which was
established by the just and necessary wars
of King William and Queen Anne, and

which went to establish a balance of power
against France, and to erect the Austrian
Netherlands into a barrier for Holland and
that side of Germany, I conceived myself
to the full as much pledged as ever. But
was this the minister's way of thinking?
What are his pretensions to be thought the
defender of the liberties of Europe when
endangered by France? If report speaks
true, when the invasion of the Austrian
Netherlands was determined upon, Mr.
Pitt caused a communication to be made
to the French ministry that they were welcome to the whole of them provided they
would agree not to touch Holland. This
fact he has never denied, although stated
in his presence in parliament more than
once. Again, when the King of Sardinia,
upon the invasion of Savoy, called upon
him to fulfill the treaty of Worms, going
out of his way as it should seem to be distinct, he flatly and positively refused it.

Under this explanation Sir, the neutrality recommended by Mr. Fox claims to
be interpreted; a neutrality, the very opposite to that which was followed, as his,
the result of resolution, would have been
accompanied by armament, and Mr. Pitt's,
the offspring of indecision, was supine
and pusillanimous. Under this explanation, coupled with the admitted capacity,
and right, of France to reform or to spoil

Q

her government, I demand judgment of the question at issue, and call upon you to pronounce which kept the nearest to our ancient system of defensive foreign policy, they who contended for the armed interference of Great Britain when the Netherlands were menaced, or Mr. Pitt who gave them up to the sword, or the fraternity of France, under the single restriction of her abstaining from an attack on Holland? You augured however, much mischief from the recognition of the republic, and much relaxation in the vigour of the royalist's exertions. First, I am entitled to ask, how did your minister second those exertions when they were made? Secondly, I have a right to argue from what we have seen, that the diminution of energy on the part of the royalists, confined to one corner, would have been more than compensated by the universal diminution of energy on that of the republicans throughout the whole, of France. It is plain that you have lost more than you have gained, by making the subject of government any part of your dispute. But is it true that by temporising with France, you would have destroyed the spirit of your cause? Could Europe never have recovered her heart, if you had once condescended to parley with this republic in the regular diplomatique form? If to recognize a title we think bad in a government, be, in reality, to destroy that

which we think good, what shall we say to
King William, who recognized the title of
Philip the Vth. to the throne of Spain, at
the very moment he was preparing for the
war of the succession? What happened
from this? Did the Duke of Marlborough
feel it's effects at Blenheim? Did he feel it
at Ramillies? Or when he was at the gates
of Lisle? Or when he had cleared his way
to the gates of Paris? Or was it until the
ignominious peace of Utrecht, negociated
under other auspices, that the *title* of Philip the Vth became of any value to him in
the eyes of Europe against his opponent?

I know this is no case of precedent: perhaps there are none in politics. But it will
not follow from hence that no use can be
made of the wisdom of our ancestors. I
would have recognized the republic of
France in the spirit in which Philip the
Vth was recognized by the best and wisest
of our Kings, that is, (and not as sophistry
may object, with a design of going to war
with her as soon as we were ready) under
the pressure of a case which made it expedient, and with the intent of reducing the
quarrel, if quarrel we must, to the safest
point for us to take issue upon. In the
case before us, the formal recognition was
nothing, the substantial recognition was
every thing; and the merits of that must
ha e depended not upon receiving, or

sending a regular minister, but upon the terms agreed upon with that minister. After having gone so far, I do not scruple to declare for myself, that if France had determined to retain her conquests, even Savoy, my vote should have gone for the war. To some indemnification I think she was entitled by the unprovoked aggression of the allied powers ; but that should have been in money, and not in the cession of so material a barrier as Savoy. You would have gained by this way of proceeding, a fixed object. You would have gained the plea of justice and necessity in the prosecution of that object. You would have been gainers on the side of enthusiasm within France. Here, you would have been gainers on that of unanimity to support the war, and vigour to conduct it. All these weapons you have blunted or thrown aside. You have raised in France "an armed nation" against you. The confusion in your objects, as Mr. Pitt has stated them, and which probably has contributed as much as any other cause to the marked disunion among the confederates, when examined with regard to it's operation in France exceeds all calculation. Hope and fear, those strongest inducements of the human mind, are in the ranks against you. By pledging yourselves to nothing distinct, you have disarmed every party in France of it's prospect to save, or to better itself by change. By setting no limit to your demands, you have put every man upon his defence; you have exalted terror into despair. You have done this for no purpose but to keep present power, and to secure future indemnity, to a minister, who is as false to you as he has been unfaithful to them. Already has he begun to measure back his steps. Already are you prepared to see him negociate with the present rulers in France in "*a cafe of extreme necessity.*" What he means by this no man can tell. He does not know himself. What in his judgment is a case of extreme necessity, the accidents of the times may produce every day. It is any thing that embarrasses his administration. He may give you a peace with France to enable him to make war with Ireland.

Your means therefore of reducing France to a condition in which she will be glad to coincide with any of your objects, have entirely failed, as far as these could derive assistance from within. You have so demeaned yourselves as to become suspected and odious to all parties there. It remains to be seen whether you can compleat the work you have so pitifully begun, by means of any foreign force which the remainder of Europe can supply. For one so full of hope, I think you are singularly circumstanced. Your vigour, that is your phrenzy,

rises with your disasters. There is something truly frightful in the last struggles
of your pride. In a fourth campaign against
France, with exhausted forces, with Holland against you, the Austrian Netherlands gone, a great part of Germany in the
possession of your enemy, with scarcely
the means of opposing her a month together in Italy, Prussia changed sides, Spain
as good as neuter if you are yet so fortu-
nate, the Mediterranean and the West In-
dies calling out to you for all your care to
make head on the defensive, the war in La
Vendeé finished, you are now undertaking
to do that which yourselves condemned,
as vain and impracticable, when the whole
of this picture was reversed. If any certain principle be to be found in the conduct
of your ministers, or in their official documents, or in their parliamentary declarations, it is, that without the assistance of
some active, and acting principle of discontent in the interior, the whole experiment was
idle. There was an end both of all power
to shake their government, and all pretence
for trying it. It was with arguments drawn
from this source, that ministers and their
friends replied to Mr. Fox whenever he
reasoned upon the absurdity of attempting
the conquest of France. I believe them.
They did not expect to conquer France;
neither had they the foresight to see that

except by her conquest, all other chance *they* had of destroying her government was vain. They are welcome to this concession. How will it serve them? Why truly it will enable them to say, we disowned this intention at first, we reprobated the scheme as the climax of folly and absurdity, but now that no other choice is left us between that and negociation, with our eyes open to all that is described to us as the state of Europe, with no army to carry into effect any chain of operations, with no means of coming into contact with France except by the infringement of neutralities certain to be the causes of more wars, with a starving, discontented people and an incapable ministry, we will now for the first time try the experiment, not of conquering France only, but of conquering Prussia, Holland, the Netherlands, all the neutral part of Germany which lies between the Austrian territories and France, and all that which is in her possession. I understand the fallacy, frequently, of what in logick is called a dilemma; but this is a dilemma of fact. The ministers have no escape. They must now avow either that they carry on the war, or to speak correctly, that they continue in a state of war, to see what chance may bring them, or that they have seriously begun to think about conquering France. They can take no one military step without some view to this object, if the war goes on upon the continent. Upon the ocean it is a war of piracy.

It were making a cruel use of your patience to combat this folly with serious argument. Believe me it is not to discuss with you the means of effecting this conquest that I wish you shortly to advert to the present state of Europe. Very different are the reasons which render that state so highly interesting. The question is no longer whether we shall *give* law to France, or whether, failing in the attempt, the members of the confederacy shall retire each quietly to his home to repair his fortune, just as if nothing had happened ; but whether by our obstinacy we are not creating and raising up a power of a new description, from which we must *receive* the law for years to come?

Amidst the general convulsions that have shaken to their centre those regular governments which took the lead in the measures to coerce France, there subsists, fortunately for some part of Europe, a strength hitherto untouched, and which is daily augmenting under the faults and follies of the rest. The Swiss republics, Sweden, Denmark, and some of the states of Italy considerable from their local importance, have wisely kept aloof from this contest, and rest upon their arms, not ingloriously, but with the

full means of securing respect to their neutrality. Every one of these powers, which it
is well worth remarking, are either pure aris-
tocracies, or under the guidance of the aristo-
cratic principle, we have exasperated in their
turns by bullying manifestoes, which when
it came to the point, we meanly and pusil-
lanimously retracted. A sense of their own
security will not suffer them to be uncon-
cerned spectators of our losses. So long
as they have reason to think us actuated by
the same sentiments and counsels which inspired those manifestoes, they will see that
their safety consists in keeping down the
power of Great Britain: and to do this effectually, all they will require is some continental power of sufficient consideration
and force to act as their head, and give
consistency to their confederacy. That
power has already stepped forth. Prussia
has made her peace with the republic of
France on the principle which best facili-
tates a confederacy of those nations which
have remained neutral during the war.
Prussia, withdrawing herself in good time
from the prosecution of a fruitless contest,
with her army entire, her resources comparatively but little diminished, offers under
the eleventh article of her treaty with
France, mediation, and peace to the German principalities on the Rhine, and under
the general spirit of that treaty, friendship

R

and alliance to all those who stand separate from the members of the present coalition.

This treaty of peace, if not counteracted
by wise counsels on our side, will extend
it's principle wider and wider every day,
until a total change is effected in the politics of Europe. First, let us consider it's
immediate consequence. It is here very
current that immediately after the signa-
ture of the preliminaries, a peremptory
order was sent to the British head quarters
to evacuate the territories of his Prussian
Majesty. Are we in a condition to dispute
the point with him? If we are, it must be
by force of arms; but if not, what military
operation can take place against France on
the side where, from every motive of our
ancient policy, we should be chiefly anxious to make an impression? Can we cross
the Rhine? Could we form the siege of
Maestricht? Is there any entrance into
Holland, or the Netherlands without passing his door? I do not know that towards
the Upper Rhine, our prospect is much
better. All the Emperor can do, perhaps,
will be to keep Mentz. If he wishes to
make that fortress a point for military
operation against France, admitting that
Prussia would allow this, he must establish
in it the whole of his magazines, and assemble there all the force he may want for his

expeditions. But when he has got them
there, what is the use of his position? Unless he can retake Luxemburgh, he cannot
attempt on that side the recovery of the
Netherlands. All he obtains by it is the
means of making predatory incursions into
the Palatinate. France is far away! But
should he once lose Mentz, to all the purposes of a war he might as well make one
upon the Emperor of China. He has not so
much as a road into France. Here the
Prussian treaty shuts him out. From the
hour he loses Mentz, all between him and
France is dead neutrality. The eleventh
article of the Prussian treaty comes directly
in force, the spirit and obvious meaning of
which is to make that monarch guarantee
of the peace to all those princes of the
empire who accept neutrality with France
through his mediation. His Prussian Majesty, as soon as he begins to act in this
character, assumes the right of interfering
to stop the march of any troops, or stores
through the territories of those princes.
The Emperor is checkmate. I shall not
fatigue you with discussing the question
whether this Emperor, consistently with
his late declaration to the diet of Ratisbon,
can continue the war as King of Hungary.
But let us admit him to be sincere both in
that rescript, and in his intention of fulfill-
ing the treaty he has just entered into with

us for his loan. By this last engagement, I will suppose him still a party to the war, and by the first declaration, at peace, as head of the empire, with France. This situation, curious in many respects, will be so in nothing more than in the way in which it bears upon the point we are considering. If, as head of the empire, he makes his peace, it is not the King of Prussia alone who will prevent his coming into contact with France; he excludes himself. The neutrality of the empire binds him with regard to all military operations on the side of Germany, to the full as much as it can bind any one of the lesser princes for whom it is stipulated. If a treaty therefore, should take place for this purpose, the spirit of that article in the Prussian peace which provides for removing the war from the North, will remove it from every other part, of Germany; and if the King of Hungary should retain any desire of coming to close quarters with France, the Emperor of Germany must embark his troops at Trieste under the convoy of a British squadron to join the British forces at Southampton; by which time it is probable that some plan of future operation will be concerted.

The next consideration is that which relates to the possession of Holland by France. I do not yet think it fair to state the reasoning which belongs to this question considered in any remote political point of view. The justice of all such speculations must depend upon the event of a peace, and whether Holland shall then be left in her present situation. But the importance of the separate peace which Holland has concluded with France, and of her occupying that counry as a military station, is a subject the most serious, and one that presses home to our immediate regard. From that moment your great continental confederacy was hamstrung. We heard a vast deal, indeed his Majesty's speech condescended to speculate in the same way, concerning the insecurity of this peace to Holland. I thought very much with the ministers. But what made it insecure? Their own conduct, in obstinately rejecting all overtures towards a general peace, and compelling Holland to take her chance for safety in a separate one. Had they been possessed of the least capacity, nay had they seriously looked forward to preserving the remnant of a confederacy against the future ambition of France, they would have begun negociating for themselves, for Holland, for the Emperor, and all the rest of the allies, while those allies were a consolidated body, and while it was yet a matter of doubt whether Pichegru could cross the Waal. The prospect of a *safe* peace for

Europe would at the least have been as pro-
mising as it became after the States General
had concluded a separate treaty, and as it
is now, when other considerable powers
are following their example. Waving however, all further remarks on this head, let
us view it in it's military relations. Holland in the hands of France gives her the
entrance of Germany on the weakest side.
From Wezel to Magdebourg there is not a
fortification to oppose to her. This was
her advantage before the Prussian treaty.
What is it since? Between them, these two
powers command the whole direct commerce of the North of Germany, and all
that is carried on circuitously through that
part of Europe with the rest of the world.
They possess all the great northern navi-
gable rivers from the Scheld to the Vistula.
If you contemplate power in the sources of
power, what a view of it is here! Yet even
this is but a pigmy representation. While
France holds Holland, the whole of your
eastern coast is at her mercy. In her hands
the station is unhappily such as to out flank
your least defensible side, as well as that of
Germany. It is not in my plan to present
you with the detail of it's naval inconveniences. You will not fail to remark however, that for upwards of a century the
naval system of this country has been shaped
and measured to the shores of France. You

will find it difficult to establish a naval arsenal in the North of Great Britain time enough to afford you protection in those seas. On the eastern coast, that is from the Foreland to Leith Roads, I learn that it is doubtful whether you can create a harbour for men of war. In the mean while your Baltic trade, the sinews of your marine, is open to your enemy's depredations. All the commerce his Prussian Majesty permits you to carry on with the North of Germany, must pass their doors.

I connect my observations on this part of the subject with the Prussian treaty, because, before that event, France could not derive it's full military advantage from the possession of Holland. It were needless to press any further the effects of that treaty upon the operations of the war. There are considerations, however, behind, of a yet more alarming import. Considering the Prussian treaty upon a larger scale, it strikes me as likely to become the foundation of a new system of national engagements coming in aid of the new system of government and manners with which the world is threatened. In this view it forms a new epoch in the French revolution. But a short time ago, the worst that Europe had to fear, was that the influx of French principles would produce, through a gradual revolution of sentiment, revolutions in all her governments: but never could it have been credited even by those who confided most in the triumph of the revolution eventually, that by a direct league with one of the most considerable of the regular governments, one half of Europe would be seen confederated to force it's principles upon the other. I think this very likely to be the case, in the present situation of affairs. If the King of Prussia had merely withdrawn himself from the war, nothing further could be said of him than that he acted like a wise Prince. But he has done more. His treaty with France has all the effect of an alliance, and must be so argued to speculate freely upon it's consequences. Now the intent of an alliance is to give effect to some purpose; and either is made in opposition to some present interest among adverse neighbouring powers, or looks forward to the possibility of it. In either case, the contracting parties must necessarily use all the means within their reach to advance the object of their alliance. What are those means on the part of Prussia? Purely military. What are they on the part of France? If we conceive her present state to continue, certainly she has not, among the various means of offensive war against herenemies, any one more important than the propagation of her opinions. I profess myself a great believer in the efficacy of peace to cure what is chiefly mischievous in those opinions; but that peace, as well as being ably negotiated in point of terms, must be general in point of operation. The separate peace, which has just been negotiated under the eyes of our improvident ministers between Prussia and France, will produce the very reverse: it will arrest the certain progress of these opinions to the grave, and once more bring them back to life and action, by putting that monarch in a situation in which he must depend on them for his support. I look, therefore, for the revival of this revolutionary phrenzy, commonly known by the name of *Jacobinism*, to the king of Prussia, and the situation in which you have put him. He it is who receives it into the bosom of Europe, and provides for it there, full freedom of action, and a permanent residence. His palace is the head quarters of its negotiators and men of business. His academies of its philosophers. Through him, the chief of a government regular beyond dispute, this enthusiastic spirit, snatched from an eternal sleep to which it had been consigned by a suffering world, obtains a direct *formal* channel of communication with other states dreadfully shortening the road to all its objects. Enlisting himself thus in its service, he becomes the centre of a new system. He proclaims himself, for the benefit of France, the great royal factor and contractor for revolutions. By his rank, power, locality, and above all, by the high degree of favour in which he stands, he forms the main link in the chain that connects her with those European states which have an interest in our humiliation. In one word, the object of the treaty he has just signed, is to place him at the head of the Germanic Empire *as the ally of France;* to give him, as the organ of the new system, a preponderance in all that relates to the government of the old, and through these means to bind up, as it were, indissolubly and for ever, the destinies of the ancient world with that of France, and to bring all its properties and its powers under the influence of her ascending constellation.

For this evil, the greatest practical evil that ever threatened us, there are none but preventive remedies : and there are no means of applying these except through a peace. It is peace alone, the occupations of peace, and the objects to which it leads, which can retard the ripening calamities of an event that opens but too surely the way to this scheme of monstrous confederation. But if you would secure this effect of peace, you must lose no time in making it. The good conduct of centuries to come may be insufficient to cure the delay of one critical month in the present posture of your affairs. A peace, or a sincere experiment for it, begun at the hour am imparting to you my thoughts, by dissolving the gigantic military fabric which France has erected, might destroy this terrible system in its first germination. What we have to fear, is that the vast irregular exertions which France has made for her defence should settle into a permanent war establishment, greater in a similar proportion, than any that can be kept up by other European governments; and this will infallibly happen if nothing intervene in her civil state, considered relatively to other nations, to divert her from carrying her views forward at the time she concludes a peace. If, therefore, you now go on with the war on the principle of changing, through its operation, the government of France, and if *ever* you come, (as you must at last) to make peace without having changed it, France must for her own sake look forward to the means of sustaining the situation in which her neighbours shall have been forced, tardily and unwillingly, to consent that she should stand. This principle opens the door to her connecting herself by treaties and alliances with those states which may be disposed to come into them, exactly upon the old scheme of the court of Versailles, but with very different means of effecting their purposes. She gets this principle by the general urgency of her situation; she gets the habits of acting upon it every day the war lasts. Reciprocal danger binds her closer to Prussia. The chain of continuity is kept up between the necessity of her present exertions, and that of settling a plan of permanent policy for foreign affairs, which embraces the question of foreign connections, and the establishments by which these are maintained. All this you would withdraw from the eyes of the people of France by any advance towards a peace, made them in the true spirit of pacification : because it is not untill then that they can begin to think of a constitution ; but the moment you set them seriously to work upon it, you give them an interest in all those benefits which are the objects of a constitution. France, for these last three years, has been living upon her principal. Half an age of retrenchment will scarcely, under the cheapest constitution they may fancy, enable her to keep within the income of her industry. But whosoever governs France, and looks but a year before him, will find that towards settling any constitution for her at all, he must call to his aid every one of the advantages of peace : that he must set out upon a plan of contracted expenditure, and of attention to resource, wholly and alike adverse to any system of foreign alliance which requires the support of a large war establishment. This brings us to the point. If that infatuated policy shall continue, which teaches the sovereigns of Europe that their safety depends

on nourishing and keeping alive the anarchy
of France, and when the horrors of war shall
have ceased by their inability to continue
them, on their adopting a system of intrigue
and cabal which shall permit no respite to
her miseries ;—if unfortunately they fall
in with the projects of those ministers,
who, to console them for their disappoint-
ments, shall pour into their ears the balmy
counsels of persecution and revenge, and encourage them with the cheering prospects of
ruined commerce, of depopulated towns, of
neglected agriculture, of returning discord,
massacre, famine and desolation, then must
we expect that France, never quiet herself,
will leave no quiet to her neighbours. If
the contrary shall prevail,—if kings at length
shall learn, that by augmenting the sum of
human happiness they provide for the certain
augmentation of their own,—if France be allowed to see, and think, that her recovery is
worth trying for, then may the elements once
more be hushed, the troubled ocean retire to
its bed, and these lowering military confederacies be dissipated for ever.

I do not tell you this will be the certain
effect of negotiation, or even of peace. All
depends on the time you choose for it. Is
this voluntary ? the chances are as certainly
in your favour as in human calculations any
thing can be so. Is it forced upon you ? I
will answer for no terms from France worth

to a manly mind the difference between them and utter annihilation. Your ministers are putting all to the hazard: I fear that under their management, any termination of our immediate evils will be but the beginning of others ten thousand times more intolerable. I repeat to you, Sir: if peace ever shall be made while the Prussian alliance with France continues in force, and *no change of system or disposition shall have taken place in this country* with regard to French affairs, you have no security for its lasting one hour. It will be a peace engendering wars by generations; and the worst of all wars, as partaking of their common stock. They will be wars not of commerce and territory, but of government and opinion.

I lament to tell you, Sir, that here we talk in a much higher tone. Nothing goes down but war, if our misfortunes are considered with any view to the repairing them. We defy augury and fate. We talk of a triple alliance; of a league, defensive as it is called, between the courts of London, Vienna, and St. Petersburgh, which is to counteract the king of Prussia's treaty with France, to crush his power, and if necessary to parcel out his dominions. According to this speculation nothing is so easy: it is but the work of a campaign. In spite of the confidence with which I hear this promised, I cannot help suspecting our enlightened age to be lamenta-

bly deficient in the art of calculating conquests. By all I can learn, or observe of
Prussia, she is likely to prove a bitter morsel
to her devouring pursuers. Hitherto we
have seen little of Prussia but her politics.
Acting with an army against France, in
concert with the irreconcileable enemy of
her dominion, her military energy has always been veiled under the cloud of a du-
bious faith. All that we know for certain
is, that in the contest from which she has
just withdrawn herself, she has suffered in
her treasure and her troops in no decent proportion to the other powers. It is generally
admitted by those best capable of forming a
judgment, that the interior of the Prussian
dominions bears less than any other country
you can visit the marks of this common calamity. In pecuniary resources she is beyond all comparison richer than either of the
continental branches of this triple confederacy. In those which belong to political
situation, the advantages are altogether as
much on her side. From the House of
Austria she has nothing directly to fear. In
the present state of Europe the chances of a
Silesian war would be rather in her favour.
It is on the side of Poland, and chiefly the
newly acquired territories, that our great
hopes of giving the law to the King of Prussia are supposed to rest.

Whatever may have been the fate of that gallant but unfortunate people, the vigour with which they resisted the last dismemberment of their country has at least proved the extent of public sentiment in Poland, and its value to any considerable neighbouring power which may find an interest in going with that sentiment. The King of Prussia has tried it both ways: First, when in concert with the British Minister, and to set up his own interest in Poland against that of Russia, he settled the new government with the leaders of the revolution in 1791. Secondly, when by the desertion of that minister in a contest in which he had embarked at his instance, he was driven into the arms of Russia, and into a participation of her views. This is the sum of his history with regard to Poland. He has had his share in the plunder of a country which, without his co-operation, never could have been plundered at all. It seems the two Imperial courts are now to deprive him of those acquisitions, and share them amongst themselves. I think they will experience a difficulty in this second transfer not so easily conquered as when they met it in the first. Perhaps the court of Vienna may find itself not altogether at ease on the side of Hungary and the Turkish frontier. But what should hinder the King of Prussia from changing sides in the politics of Poland, and coming

round again to the revolutionists of 1791?
What should hinder him, after having secured
his own share of the spoil by stipulations
which they who remain in Poland would be too
wise to refuse complying with, from march-
ing a Prussian and a French army into the
heart of the Russian provinces, and with the
aid of its inhabitants, wresting the whole of
them out of her hands ? You talk of extir-
pating the King of Prussia through Poland.
It is on this side the Russian empire is chiefly vulnerable herself; and never, depend
upon it, while the wise counsels prevail
which have governed that court for so many
years, never will any step be taken to disturb
the *happy compromise* which extended her dominion last year to the banks of the Vistula.
The speculation is extravagant.

The state of our account, therefore, I take
to be all to nothing against us. I wish no
man so ill as that he should employ himself
in examining it with a view either to the conquest of France, or to any change in her will
with regard to the fort of government she is to
set up. It is to little purpose that Mr. Windham, and others of his way of thinking, have
obtained at last some share in the counsels under which the war is managed. They come
to a government exhausted by adventurous
improvidence, and stand before a people fa-
tigued, discouraged, querulous, and full

T

charged with the materials of a most frightful discontent. The time was gone by either for honest advice, or vigorous action.
Your war had got such an ill name, that no
wisdom, no spirit, no honourable pledge of
their persons or characters could restore it.
I have dwelt the longer upon these matters,
and gone the more into details relative to the
origin of our misfortunes, from a desire of
standing clear with you in those points
which relate to the separation of our old
friends, as well as from an anxiety, which I
cannot help feeling as a matter of taste, that
the original ground of their difference with
us should not be confounded with those we
are now contending with Mr. Pitt. To
these I will add a yet stronger motive; for
neither shall the character of our party
survive its fate, nor can the country look
with any hope towards its preservation,
unless we determine upon a retrospective in-
quiry into the conduct of the war, in order
to fix the blame of our discomfitures where
it is due. It is not for us to be told by a
minister, with an easy accommodating levity,
" We have tried one scheme and failed ;
" now let us all be friends, and try an-
" other ;"—this is not the way to act with
dignity or effect. If an effort is to be made
for our country, and surely it deserves one,
we must know who are willing, and who are
able. A great change in your situation is at

hand. With dispositions in government less pacific than ever, possibly you are not very distant from a peace with France. Great as you may suppose the evil, it must come at last. With peace, you must have intercourse; you must be civil to this republic of Jacobins, reared by the hands of Jacobins of the worst order, if disdain and horror will admit of your distinguishing them. You must bethink yourselves of making some provision for this eventful change; for eventful indeed it will be, and whether to our prosperity or to our ruin, must wholly depend upon those who are at the head of affairs in the moment of its arrival. Whence it is to proceed, whether from inability to go on with the war, or from the exhausted patience of the people calling for new measures and new men, I will not pronounce, but some there must be, else there will be nothing left to change except your government. You may now choose, and do not undervalue this great privilege, whether you will begin it yourselves, or wait until it come upon you. Remember it can be done but once; but that it cannot be done at all, unless you place each man in the rank and station proper for him to accomplish the purposes of such a change. If you neglect this, you will be as much in the dark with regard to the circumstances on which it is to operate, as you have been hitherto with regard to the objects for which all your prosperity has been risqued. Every thing will be thrown back upon that capricious discretion which you vainly fancy yourselves to be fixing and confining by the resolution to adopt any change at all, until at last you will discover that you have consumed by anticipation whatever you had a right to hope for from the frugal and the proper use of this last resource.

Taking it, therefore, for granted as a point of mere dry fact, that one of these days, and not very distantly perhaps, you must make peace with a republic of some sort in France; we shall not differ, I think, in this, that it must be our care to guard our own government from the shock, if any shall be to be feared, of the recognised subversion of monarchy in so extended a portion of the civilised world. Observe, Sir, that if I can by any means consent to admit the possibility of our preservation from the dangers that immediately surround us, I must caution you against setting it down to aught of a temper very common amongst us, and in an equal degree sanguine and indolent, by which men buoy themselves up with ideas of our boundless resources, and other general fancies of the like sort, and about as solid. No step that I take, none that I would advise, is determined upon any such expectation. But you have not yet restored me to the full freedom of despair. Where little is left for hope, much may remain for duty, which, in these cases, travels on beyond hope, and never fairly leaves us till the last. That duty tells me that we must attempt the adventure in all its ways. I neither promise you that a peace is to be had; nor that, if obtained, it could save us; but I think we ought to try for it; and in recommending it, I have a right to press upon your adoption all that may be necessary to make the experiment successful. Otherwise, with every expectation from peace, and my sincere good wishes for it generally speaking, I am by no means sure that the present minister may not conclude one which will be yet worse than his war. We may consider this point further by-and-by; I mention it for the present to avoid the difficulty with which they would embarrass us, who desire nothing better for themselves than the inertness of despair in good minds. Whatever may be our chance, better or worse, we must try it, and make the best we can of it. Impressed with this feeling, I have bestowed a little more attention than perhaps a wiser man would think it right to waste, upon the means which are left to extricate ourselves. The speculation, it is merely such, leaves me I own very much a prey to fears of all kinds. I am afraid that, to any good purpose, the change, as well as being more sudden, must be far more extensive than we are yet prepared for.

We have been fed too high with provocatives to return with any relish to the plain wholesome food of our ancestors. Calamity has come upon us with too hasty a stride. Some hours should have been snatched from the tomb, and allotted us for meditation and repentance. We retain, I doubt, yet too great a hankering after our old sins to take up new courses, and, by a sincere contrition for the past, deserve to be received once more within the pale of the constitution. I question whether we have time, I cannot trust to our inclination, for any work of permanent prospective good.

If we are to try peace without such dispositions, better were it perhaps to be wholly passive. Whatever is undertaken, I am sure cannot admit of being thwarted in its progress by any intermixture of their opposites. Indeed, I scarcely know what one conciliatory exertion we can dispense with in providing for the complicated objects which are included in my idea of a peace. All the considerations belonging to it are of the highest order in politics. To be any thing less than an evil, peace must be established, or attempted, in a spirit widely different from any that has hitherto seemed to influence the conduct of your ministers. Very serious will be the matter of its terms and formal stipulations; but, viewing a peace with France as connected with our future situation under it; with the part we must act, and the share which will belong to us under the new system of Europe ; with the evil or the good which we may be made to derive from it by wife, or weak counsels; with the alliances we must contract; with the establishment of that sort of plan and system of home administration which may alternately conciliate and repress, according to the dictates of a steady, liberal, and manly policy ; with the renewal of a dreaded inter-course, so impossible to avoid if we have peace at all, so essential to our commerce, and through that to the re-establishment of our resources ;—viewing it, Sir, in all these relations, it is scarcely possible to fill the mind with conceptions of a more elevated nature than are included in this one word Peace. This will be no naked question of territory, but a great settlement, practically involving in its consequences all those ques-tions which I have ever thought your eager-ness for alarm has so imprudently antici-pated. It will depend upon the capacity and honesty of those who negotiate it, whe-ther from the signing of its articles any traces of this old world of our's shall remain, or whether a new scheme of things, leading to other customs, other morals, other social connections, the reverse of all our present ones, will not take their date; whether in short the evils too hastily predicted from

attempting to negotiate in an early stage,
when your power was whole, will not happen in a later when you carry negotiation
into effect with your power destroyed. Such
a measure, you will see at once, requires
the utmost liberty of action, and for this
end the movers in it must be endowed with
the largest portion of our confidence. I
have great doubts whether your minister is
a man equal to this arduous undertaking.
I am sure he is not likely, through any sug-
gestion of his own, to consult the necessities
of the country, and enter fairly into such measures. I will submit to you my reasons for so
thinking, in a few short observations on some
of the leading objects just enumerated.

In the first place, I cannot expect from
Mr. Pitt, (except in one view which shall
speedily be noticed,) any sincere renunciation
of the project of destroying the French government.. Until this be done, not in words
but in fact, not by ministerial professions,
but by national engagements, all expectations
of peace are idle and illusory. Do not think
I mean to charge him with that inveteracy
of consistency which would restrain a man
who had ventured upon the lofty language
towards France which he has used, from
being a party to a measure which, coming
from him, must be taken as an apology for
it. Verily I acquit him of all such unpro-
fitable stubbornness. Neither can I believe

I

him to flatter himself any longer with the hope of success in the war itself. He can expect as little as you or I, that foreign arms can unmake the republic, or if you will, the Jacobinism of France; or that any individual would long escape the kind vigilance of his next of kin who should hold in sober sadness the ostensible language of his administration. This he must know and feel; but to renounce the project, and recognize his error at the same time, the only way in which he can render repentance beneficial, were an effort of magnanimity only within the compass of men of a tried and steady principle. No good is to be looked for from the renewal of a negotiation similar to that carried on before the rupture with M. Chauvelin. Such a measure would be dishonourable and delusive to both parties. They who are entrusted with this nice business, must begin by renouncing for themselves and their allies, all confederacies for the purpose of imposing a government on France. That question must be set at rest in the first instance, or your negotiation cannot advance a step. You must do this, were it only to tie up your hands from tearing off your bandages in a moment of returning phrenzy, and again setting the fountain of your blood at play. But while you thus bind yourselves, which in your present state would be an advantage to you, you bind France too. Is it

U

nothing think you, to set this question, in
which success and power will assert so large
an interest, totally aside in all discussions
between you and France? In the hour of
your insolence you raised against treating with
her, an objection of principle. What should
prevent France in the hour of her success,
from throwing a similar impediment in the
way of accommodation with you? You rejected negotiation with her, because you
could not trust her government.   Why
should not she reject a treaty with you
as well for what she cannot, as what she
can, trust in yours?   Unless you recall those
volumes of manifestoes with which you have
covered Europe, France cannot trust to your
stipulations ; but she can trust, if experience
be worth any thing, to the general feeling of
your government for its seizing the first favourable moment to renew the war.   The
present minister can give you no security
for attending to the adjustment of a point in
so many views indispensable. In fact, by
separating the question of government from
the terms of peace, as a preliminary, he would
do precisely what Mr. Fox recommended
two months before hostilities commenced ;
and however sincerely you may conclude him
disposed to adopt any measure which secures
him in his place, it is not in human credulity,
after the conduct you have witnessed two
short years ago, to believe that in recog-

nizing the French republic he will be actuated by those considerations, which, both in then, and in every succeeding circumstance of the country, made that a measure of prudence, which is now becoming a measure of hard and afflicting necessity.

Depend upon it, Sir, that to this point of recognition, of naked, unqualified, previous recognition, we must eventually arrive " The disgrace, and the necessity of yielding it, grow upon us every day." Instead of making it, as we pretended to do with America, the price of peace, we must, as by that unfortunate war we were compelled, begin by recognition, and discuss the terms by themselves. It is only thus that we can make peace; it is only thus, let me add, that we can make legitimate war; for so long as we refuse to negotiate under the pretence that the republic is something we have a right to give to France, or to withhold from her, or to clog with conditions and compromises, disguise it under what diplomatique subtleties you will, it is the government which is the object of the war, not incidentally as the means of repelling the aggression of an enemy, but directly as the means of gratifying those passions which produced it.

Such must be their conduct who look for peace on truly pacific principles. You are not one from whose " uncandid dulness" I have much to fear in making use of this

phrase. You will not suspect that in striving
to guard what remains of British empire
and constitution from the destructive ignorance of those who take the lead in your
councils, my only purpose is to surrender it
to a French committee of safety. How you
will decide on any question, is what I cannot
venture to anticipate; but with regard to this
which divides us, I feel that at length the
time is come when you will bear to be told
that at least you must examine it upon its own
merits, and that you must cease to encumber
it with the difficulty of fixing any such motives upon those who deprecated the war from
its commencement, and forewarned you of
its event. You will see, what the tenor of my
whole life shall justify against these praters
about the constitution, that by urging you to
search for peace in the spirit of peace, I
mean nothing so little as to recommend to
you the example of France at any one period
since the revolution ; that I afk for no more
than a fair, honourable termination of this
unavailing contest. Certainly after what has
passed, I cannot expect this from Mr. Pitt.
Even were he disposed to attempt it, there
are many reasons which render it impoffible
for him to open a negotiation for peace upon
any honourable footing, to obtain even tole-
rable conditions, or to provide any solid security for its preservation.

First, as to the point of honour: I mean
of the national honour; for with regard to
what is due to his individual character, as
far as in great public transactions that can
admit of separation from the character of
the state under whose authority he acts, he
must be left to his own feelings, such as
they are. Among the many causes of this
war, whether of its origin or its continuance is no matter, Mr. Pitt has uniformly
placed in the first rank his fear, or his dislike, or call by what name you will, his
objections to the principles on which France
pretends to found her Republic. This Republic, or government, or anarchy, which-
soever you please, he has attempted to
overturn by force; and he has failed. The
attempt, however, was made by him as representing the sentiments of this country,
whose honour, notwithstanding every misfortune of the war with America, was delivered safe, whole, and unimpaired into his
hands. Is it possible, Sir, that admitting
his readiness to crawl in the dust before
France after having talked so big on this
side of the British channel—is it possible
that, as an Englishman, I can consent to see
my country submit to that last of degrada-
tions—that of retracting all its vain and
arrogant pretensions through the very
mouth that uttered them? If I pass an insult upon any man in the face of the world,

honour requires that he should compel me
to retract it in the same mode and form as
that in which it was given. There can be
no compromise. He who has received it
is at liberty to go no where else for relief
but to me. That identical portion of character which I have taken from him, he
must tear from mine, and mine only. For
me there is as little choice. Poor of spirit
indeed is he who speculates upon a middle
course. I am not fond, in general, of ana-
logies between cases of individuals, and
cases of governments; but in this before us
the parallel holds exactly, as it will in all
questions of government which go to their
legitimacy. To dispute this, is in the very
highest order of insult. Now, Sir, without
going into abstract considerations of the
legitimacy of that of France, I ask, are you
in a condition to dispute it with her? But
did not Mr. Pitt dispute it with her? and
can he now, or under any circumstances,
recognize that legitimacy without renouncing for us, as a nation, all those high sentiments through which, appealing to our
pride, our honour, and our feelings, he engaged us to deny it, and to support that denial by trying our strength with France
upon the very point? This were an abject
suing for peace,—this were, indeed, to bow
down the head of Britain, and cover it with
indecorous dust. All advances towards

I

France on the part of Mr. Pitt, must necessarily be so many apologies for his arrogance, not in his name, but in your's.

It is not the mere indecency of this which
would disgust me. It is a point that goes
to essentials; influencing very considerably
on the terms of any treaty we might conclude with France; and as vitally connected
with our honour, affecting through that our
security for every thing else. France, in
treating with Mr. Pitt, must naturally take
into consideration all the circumstances
which create in him a readiness to treat with
her. In the first place, she knows his disposition; how far she may trust to the sincerity of his pacificatory professions; how
far he is likely to abstain from giving her
any disturbance after peace by meddling
with her parties and factions. Giving her
credit for what degree of moderation you
will, you must be sure that France, if she
acts wisely, will weigh all these considerations; that she will calculate her risque in
the terms of her agreement; that these terms
will be higher, or lower, in proportion to
what she will have to apprehend from the
hostile, or treacherous disposition of the
power with whom she negotiates. Believing that he seeks in a peace, nothing
but a suspension of hostilities, in order to
renew the war at a more favourable moment,
she will think it right to secure herself

against the effects of a surprize, by insist-
ing in some instances upon cessions, in
others upon renunciations, which to us
may appear in the highest degree exorbi-
tant; but which, to speak truth, would be
no more so than we, under the same circumstances, should conceive ourselves entitled to ask from her. This, you will say,
is putting a very extreme case; and supposing that France will have it in her power
to dictate to us what peace she likes. I do
not see how your objection is to remove
the probability of the fact. If Mr. Pitt
continues minister, I most certainly think
that it will be so. France has measured his
powers, and very much do I doubt whether
she has found any thing in them to discourage her most extravagant demands.
What countenance, I ask you, can he wear
towards France, by whom he has been so
beaten into a sense of his incapacity, except
that of the most abject humility? In discussing the articles of peace, at what concession, however disgraceful, could he stop?
Put the most extravagant case you can think
of. He must either concede the terms, or
fight to procure better. If he concedes them,
there is an end, you will admit, of the question one way; and yet, since the experience
France has had of his abilities as a war
minister for the two first campaigns and
the beginning of the present, with what

hope of intimidating her could he resort to
measures of vigour and resolution? What
cares France either for his manifeftoes, or
for his armies, or, notwithstanding British
superiority, what cares she even for his
navies? Would she understand his determination of renewing the war as a threat, or
an invitation?

It is not, therefore, to peace on honourable terms, but to peace on any terms, that
we must prepare ourselves to submit, if
we leave the present minister to negotiate it.
I cannot bear to impart to you all my fears on
this subject. I would not put into the heads
of our enemies the hundredth part of the
conceffions I think him disposed to make.
It is perfectly true what you suggest with
regard to the difficulty both of settling the
terms of peace, or providing for its duration, in the present posture of affairs. No
man will deny it, but he to whose presumption and self-sufficiency all things are alike
easy. The negotiator of such a treaty must
bring to it the firmest courage, the most
comprehensive genius and sagacity, the most
enlarged knowledge of Europe and her interests, added to the most disinterested public spirit that ever were combined in man.
Rejecting all imaginary dangers, it will be
his to foresee the real ones connected with
the establishment of this vast military Republic, and to prevent her, if yet it can be

X

prevented, from drawing within her circle any very considerable European power, whose accession to her system might overbalance the rest. His will be the task to choose out for the future allies of this country, those who are best calculated to give him the great *desideratum* of a security for the peace he negotiates. His must be those talents for conciliation, that ability to inspire confidence, that temper and vigilance, which must assemble and keep together, ready to be called out at a moment's warning, all that shall be found to remain of the power and resources of Europe; and his the penetration that must discern, and the courage that must determine, the moment beyond which peace cannot be retained with safety. A minister of expedients is no minister for these objects. There is a degree of extent and combination in any rational plan of a peace for Europe under its present circumstances, which no one can even conceive, who is not a statesman upon system. It is because I think Mr. Pitt the very last you can name to me who can provide, or preserve, the securities on which peace must depend, that I object to his making it. For what is our security, and what our chance of independence, while Holland remains in the hands of France? Bad enough, you will say; but still not wholly desperate so long as other considerable states re-

main not subject to her power. If we cannot exactly balance that power, we must
do our best towards it, and collecting all
the fragments of disjointed Europe, throw
them into the opposite scale, to make what
weight they can. Confederacies, it is true,
just at this hour, are in bad repute; but although confederacies to give France a government against her will, have made but a
sorry figure, they may succeed better when
directed to better objects, and certainly are
not to be rejected from any scheme of opposing some barrier to her universal dominion. But any such confederacy, whether
to deserve success, as I may think, or to in-
sure it, as you and every body else will acknowledge, must resemble the present as little as possible, both in its objects and in the
principles of its combination. Setting aside
all objections which may lead to dispute
with respect to the present confederacy
against France, and stating the one on which
I am speculating, as simply intended to resist her force; and speaking of such, as I
always must, as a confederacy in which
Great Britain ought to take the lead, I aſk
how, or with whom it is to be formed, if
Mr. Pitt continues to direct your councils?
Who believes in his sincerity? What is the
opinion of his abilities? I would risque the
whole of the argument upon his general
estimation in the different courts with which

he has had any dealings. Spain, Austria,
Prussia, Sweden, the Porte, Russia, the
miserable, betrayed, and ruined Poland, all
will tell you within the short space of four
years, that he seemed in his foreign politics
to have no other object, or occupation than
to insult the weak, to bend before the proud,
to deceive the confiding, and every where
to stir up insurrections and rebellions,
embroiling subjects with their sovereigns,
and sovereigns with one another. Which
of these powers, do you imagine, he will be
able to engage in any system that requires
stability and a permanent trust? And how
by their means, or any of them, will he be
able to shew that best and only security for
peace, namely, that he is in a condition to
maintain it? All, in my apprehension, pronounce him unfit for the large duties we
require of a minister, who, after a peace, is
to preside over the interests of Europe as
connected by wise alliances with our own.

What do I deduce from this? Is it mere
calumny, think you, or stated only for
the purpose of invidious comparison? If
it be calumny, the worst of all calumnia-
tors are his colleagues, since it is from
them, through their example, and their
arguments, that I have chiefly been led to
form my general opinion of the transactions
of his foreign policy. The truth is, that
like all vain men, who have the misfortune
to step young, and at once, into high and

efficient offices, he has been obliged to learn his business by experiments. Observation had given him nothing, and he was too proud for counsel. The precarious tenure of his power, founded on no settled principle of public good, representing no mass of public interests, deriving force from the destruction of opinion instead of from opinion itself, was obliged to live by the day, and help itself on by one expedient or another, to the total exclusion of all objects that required time or steadiness for their completion. Himself of no description, the exigencies of his situation have obliged him to have recourse to men of all descriptions. Power of this nature whenever it fails to see its way, which it can very seldom, drives every thing to confusion, from which only it can hope to reap some benefit. Unable to stand alone, as being wholly without resource, it naturally connects itself with its next neighbour, or with the strongest for the time being that may happen to want its cooperation. This principle of present convenience, and no other, guides and influences all its movements. I do not know how better to exemplify what I am stating, if you will enlarge the scale, than by a view of the general politics which seem to influence the court of Berlin. Prussia was a power, under the old system, which the policy that governed it very clearly saw could not stand alone, and without the support of some of the powers of, what is called, the firſt order. In the year 1787 the present Sovereign entered, and wisely if wise counsels had prevailed among us, into a close connexion with Great Britain and Holland. In that of 1791 the dispute with Russia broke out. It is well known that in the settlement of that dispute to which Mr. Pitt agreed, the King of Prussia *had no voice*; that on the contrary, he considered himself outraged and betrayed by it. In faċt from that moment no alternative was left him, if he wished to keep his rank in Europe, but an alliance either with France, or with his formidable neighbour with whom we had provoked him to quarrel. Why he did not choose the first, which possibly would have been in his situation the wiser, is a wide question into which I will not enter. It is enough that we knew he could not, because we knew of the detestable negotiations going on about this time at Pillnitz, and the degree to which he was a party to them. It follows then, that either he must have stood single in Europe after the desertion of Great Britain, or have adopted the other part of the alternative; which it was also clear he could not do without consenting to participate in the views of Russia with regard to Poland. He did this. A very few months after the settlement of the Oczakoff dispute, *and in*

confequence of that fettlement, those engagements were announced between his Prussian Majesty and the Empress, which led,
as we have seen, to the plunder and destruction of Poland. In his situation, the
King of Prussia had no other choice. To
have kept him honest, he should have been
kept secure; he should not have been exposed to the temptation of alarm. This was
his conduct in 1791, in the politics of the
North. When we consider it with regard to
France from that period until his peace with
her, the same fluctuating inconsistency will
be found uniformly to distinguish it. You
never could trust him for a month together.
At one moment he was denouncing fire and
the sword against the spirit of Jacobinism,
and negotiating with it the next. Popular
opinion attributed all this to his personal
character. I own, Sir, that it struck me as
more applicable to his political situation;
precarious at all times, but rendered yet more
so by knowing that among those with whom
he was to act in close and intimate concert,
and for whom he was to brave very considerable risques, he was to number the British
cabinet. Remember, Sir, that I am offer-
ing you nothing by way of justification for
his conduct. All I mean is to shew you
how a Monarch must necessarily act who
has to keep together a species of predatory
Monarchy formed out of the odds and ends

3

of Europe, and which can exist no longer
than while it is in a state of military activity
or preparation. You now see that he has
made his peace with France. Between a
peace and an alliance with her in his case
there can be no difference.

Thinking as I do, that a very near analogy may be traced out between the principle
on which the Prussian Monarchy depends,
when we consider it relatively to the other
great kingdoms of Europe, and that which
prevails in Mr. Pitt's administration, I am
very apt to think, that if you suffer him to
negotiate at all, he will follow that Sovereign's example. Unable to give you the
real securities for peace, he will be obliged
to substitute those which are false and hol-
low. Instead of a strong foreign confederacy,
he will present you with a French alliance.
Now let me afk you, Sir, whether you are
prepared for this sort of connection with
such a neighbour? For one, I must acknowledge myself not to be fo by any means;
and beg to put in my claim to the distinction, which I trust to be wide indeed, between a peace which shall leave France to
the formation of her own government, and
that which involves an engagement of this
nature. I shall press the subject no farther
for the present, hoping that the little I have
said may put you upon your guard against

all endeavours to surprise your assent into such a proposition.

I think therefore, Sir, that the very extensive change which muft take place in your whole series of measures before you can obtain the full benefits of a peace, cannot be the work of that minister to whom you owe the war, and its train of misfortunes and disgraces; that he could not attempt negotiation with honour; that were he to conclude any pacification, its terms would be so bad as to necessitate, possibly, the breach of them on our parts; and that in the opposite case, he could provide you no security for its duration on that of France. If there be indeed, any danger that an immediate peace would bring about a revolution with us, it can only arise from a peace negotiated under such auspices, in which either a foundation would be laid for future wars againſt the government of France, or, for the sake of evading present difficulty, engagements contracted with her leading to an intercourse of politics the most hazardous. I now come to a consideration, perhaps the most serious of any. Granting all obstacles to be for the present overcome, and Mr. Pitt to settle your peace, what is to be his plan of domestic government after peace? If the end of this war be such as to bring our constitution into jeopardy, first, from the contagious influence of French princi-

ples, and secondly, by leaving France with
such large means to enforce them, it is clear,
that henceforth we must consider our constitution as one and the same thing with our
empire. Disposed to think as highly of our
constitution as any man, I have always held
that the chief part of its excellence, and the
whole of its security, depended, as the best of
human institutions must, upon the method
of administering it. I never was a favourer
of those fanciful theories of balanced
powers, sometimes mutually aiding, sometimes counteracting each other, but always
harmonizing at last. This constitution,
highly as we all prize it, can no more
support itself by its own mere spirit than
any power in mechanics can act of itself.
It is hence that very rare endowments are
requisite in a minister who aims at so
high a trust as that of giving it its impulse,
or presiding over its safety. Whatever he
may possess of zeal, vigilance, or acuteness,
will be useless, if not worse, without a
thorough and particular knowledge of the
species of mischief he will have to provide
against, and resources for repelling it derived
from long and settled constitutional habits of
action. You would not take a physician,
notorious only for his skill in poisons, and
for his readiness to give them, in the hope
that if you paid him his price he would administer to you nothing but wholesome me-
dicine. It is not by incantations and for-

ceries that the spirit of evil can be cast out.
To be a fit guardian and defender of the
constitution it is indispensable that they for
whom, and in whose name, he acts, should
agree with him as to what that constitution
is; what is its strength, and where its
weakness; what are its beauties, where its
defects; and which are its true securities.
These he muft not only keep in due repair,
and readiness for service, but possess the fa-
culty of bringing them into action at once,
and thus, on any great emergency, be able
to play off the whole resources of the state at
the same instant.

Such muft be the qualities of your minister. But what is to be the system ? Or
is government to go on, as it has hitherto, without system, upon mere temporary shifts and expedients ? Whatever
ministers may wish, they must not expect that much will be left to their option.
Look, I entreat you on France; after
having given herself a constitution, not on
your principles but her own, and maintained
at the point of the sword her will to change
and alter all things belonging to it according
to her fancy, now erected and consolidated
into one vast republic. If, when kept at a
distance by our fears, and struggling with
all the difficulties of her revolution, our danger from her opinions was such as to justify
whatever our great men have said and done

to repress them, what hope will be left us
when France, cloathed in the double fasci-
nation of novelty and victory, comes to demand an intercourse with you on terms of
conciliation and commerce? Is it just then
that these opinions will lose their danger,
and that our constitution may be left to take
care of itself? or is it upon a peace that we
are to enforce the system of *Tory terrorism*
with renovated vigour, and carry into yet
wider effect the set of measures which it has
originated? If, consistently with a state of
peace, we cannot continue our alien act, our
traiterous correspondence act, and the rest
of the laws and regulations we passed in the
same spirit against France, are we, with a
view of producing their ends in another way,
to search into the sore and tender parts of
our constitution, enact new treason laws,
and, perhaps, repeal the habeas corpus act
altogether? These are measures which,
with all the infatuation of the present day,
I scarcely should believe in the contemplation of any set of men. Yet your present
ministers have no choice; either they must
have recourse to some such, or, by doing
nothing, confess their whole conduct hitherto to have been rank imposition. If
peace with France, or even neutrality, was
so dangerous in 1793 that war, with all
its hazards, was considered as a safe experiment in comparison; and if, after trying

war, they find the danger from that so much greater, although of another sort, as to drive them back again to peace, to what a degree must not the original dangers of peace be augmented in their minds, when we consider the circumstances under which we shall come to it, and the sort of terms we are likely to obtain ? What follows in reason ? If the strong measures I have alluded to were right at a period so little flattering to the expectations of France, how infinitely more urgent will be the obligation of acting upon them when the peace shall be settled ? There seem to be no modes within the known line of the constitution of protecting it by a temporary suspension of its functions, strong enough for the necessity of their argument.— It must be abrogated at once, in form, and substance.

I am far from carrying to this extent, which must call as you will observe for still severer restraints upon public liberty, the dangers from this republic of France left in quiet possession of so many means of annoying us ; but no man will tell me that this mighty change, produced by such mighty efforts, will not oblige us, as a means of keeping our ground, to draw very largely upon the fund of our constitution. Observe, Sir, this is no constrained admission from me of an adverse argument ; it is the strong part of my case. Whether the

conclusion of the war shall leave France with
a government good or bad, it can never be
to us a matter of indifference : if it be good,
we must guard against whatever it may possess of real temptation ; if bad, against its
false pretences and its power, against its
fraud and its force. In either case I think it
high time to look about us, to muster our
whole strength, and examine what we shall
have to trust to whenever we come in the
face of mankind to a fair trial between the
value of their government and our's. Fully
satisfied with my own, I wish to give it all
advantage in this trial ; I wish it to receive
no detriment from the wickedness of its ministers, or the discontents of its subjects.
These considerations have drawn my attention very much to the quarter in which I
apprehend our chief danger to lie. If I venture to expose your weak parts, I shall do it,
Sir, with all the freedom of an old friend,
to whom it is permitted to offer wholesome
correctives, and the common remedies, perhaps with little hope of your adopting them
in time, but with as little fear from the sort
of reproach which it is so much the fashion
to throw out against the motives of such as
recommend them.

In the very first and foremost rank, I
place a spirit of perfect carelessness among
the people themselves, on all matters which
regard their pride, honour, safety, liberty, or
whatever else you can suppose in a public

point of view dear or valuable to a nation.
I think the worse of this, from observing
with what inveteracy it is attached to, and
woven in with, the scheme of our civil administration in all its branches. I am convinced that in times of danger there will be no
safe reliance on this spirit, either for the
whole of your constitution, or for any of its
parts, even for the monarchy which it seems
most to favour. I could know far better
how to deal with a stiff, high-flying monarchical spirit, which the experience of our
history tells me is to be softened and pared
down to the true standard of our constitution, for the sake of what it most loves and
venerates. Something is always to be accomplished with the pride of an independent
aristocracy. Nor should I tremble to behold
a plain, manly, genuine republican sentiment,
were it mixed with republican manners and
virtues, prevailing among the lower orders. I
find no fault with these abstractedly considered; because a wise government will always
know what to engraft on such dispositions,
and how to turn them to the general benefit.
But far different is it with the sad and name-
less jumble of all principle we see before us!
It is not that ministers are ambitious, parliaments corrupt, the crown holding its pre-
rogative too high;—such are the vices of all
ages, never to be cured, but always to be
balanced; but we seem in our public morals

to unite every opposite corruption of the extremes of mixed monarchy. The spirit of
these times is a spirit of persecuting political
bigotry, which exhibits the law upheld by
mobs, and slavery enforced by sedition. Is
it now, principally, that lofty sentiments of
honour ought to be cherished and cultivated
almost to a degree of romance; that we
should be tenacious in the extreme of privileges originating from that source; that we
should give to property even more than its
due consideration and weight; that we should
display justice in all those energies with
which she protects the good and terrifies the
bad? The duties corresponding to these
maxims shall be set before us in the sub-
limest precepts of philosophy and reason.
In vain!--Comes there a call upon our practice,
—find we the least ruggedness in our path to
make us toil and stumble, at once we desist
from the pursuit. Rich iniquity, turning
the weapons of virtue against her own breast,
claims and obtains immunity from crime
through the fruits of that crime itself: aristocracy, preserving all its insolence and none
of its pride, leagues with the court to destroy
and quench the vital spark through which
it holds a separate existence, the opinion of
its independence and of its justice: the court,
fixed beyond all precedent in the exercise of
those powers which seem rather to belong
to arbitrary, than to mixed monarchies, in-

2

capable of giving any shape or system to its
councils, lays itself out to flatter the passions
of a debauched and giddy populace; that
populace, hating the very name of liberty,
degrades and ostracises every man who seeks
to guard it upon any permanent principle of
action; the ministers, participating in this
common nature, than which for the purposes of government nothing can be so fatally
feeble, follow at an humble distance the fancy
of the day, without ever daring to lead public
opinion. This, Sir, is our state. Court, people,
ministers, all encourage one another in the
perversion of every principle of just government. Think you that this can produce
harmony? By no means: never was that
happy state intended to arise out of such
agreements. Domestic discord, in its direct
form, lurks beneath the smile of this treacherous affability. What the habit may turn
to, what fungus this rottenness may throw
out, baffles all rational conjecture. Great
power, under the dominion of great fear,
has recourse to strange expedients. If you
ask me my opinion, I should tell you, that
it would probably end in establishing among
us a revolutionary mob government, just as
bad as what they have got in France.

Do you remember the riots of Birmingham? I know there are those who express
a very high degree of exultation whenever

Z

mention is made of the transactions of those foul days. With some expressions of decent regret, and even this not very often, for the outrages then committed, such as the burning of houses, the pillage and destruction of property and of the labours of science, they think the spirit of what they call loyalty there manifested, fit matter for triumph and congratulation. Could the whole people but be animated with similar zeal, nothing would be to be feared from the progress of French revolutionary maxims; instead of declining, they would provoke the conflict. This is the language; and miserably are they deceived who hold it. Be assured that there is an end of all effective force in the law, and consequently of all certain obedience to it, when it is left to find its own level and balance between the violence of two opposing anarchies. The weakness of government stands revealed, when any class of its citizens, even those who pretend to wish it best, shall be suffered in any case whatever to flatter themselves that, by breaking through the known and fixed fences of justice they may advance its ends, and serve the constitution. Admit the danger, and you go a great way towards weakening the government; but it will begin to verge fast to its dissolution indeed when the impression shall be such among its friends, as that the established authorities are insufficient for its protection without pressing upon the last spring, and opening the reservoir of public force existing ultimately in the people, and never to be touched but in the last agonies of the state. A mob of affection is just as dangerous as a mob of disaffection. Nor is there after all, any such great difference between the mobs of Birmingham, and the mobs of Paris. The common apology of rashness belongs to neither. Our Englishmen are not so fond of blood indeed ; they are content with persecution. But the pretexts, and the purposes of each are exactly the same. Each, for the sake of justice, begins by destroying law. These restraints removed, they are left to pursue their own inclination and bent, which in all mobs, ever was, and ever will be alike. Tired of fighting against each other, they join to indemnify themselves with the common plunder of the state.

Such are not the dispositions out of which I should hope to oppose any thing durable to France in the way of example. An administration founded upon these dispositions, therefore, and encouraging their prevalence, cannot be a fit or proper depositary of the public force. What answer, indeed, can I find to all the plausible part of the French theories, from Mr. Pitt's government considered in its practice? To begin for instance, with hereditary monarchy. The French, and

Z 2

some English after them, call it an absurdity, because wisdom is not hereditary. I answer, that no English monarch governs by his own wisdom be it ever so great; that if he could, there would be an end of our liberties. It is for this reason that the constitution declares he can "do no wrong;" because he is supposed to act by the advice of his ministers, who not only can do wrong, but who can be made to smart for it. But if selfish persons about the crown, sheltering themselves under this maxim, and taking advantage of a high Tory spirit among the people, and of a disposition to interpret it in a literal, and not a virtual sense, can contrive to vest the chief offices of state in persons of no weight or consideration in the country for talents, integrity, property, or general character of any kind, and persuade the House of Commons to give to all such appointments as often as they may happen, their countenance and good will, then undoubtedly the chief argument which reconciles it to sound wisdom, namely, that the advisers of the crown who are to answer for its acts are themselves most interested in giving good advice, becomes nugatory; then it would indeed be more consonant to reason that a king should govern without any advice; and then I should be compelled to confess, which is the point to which the enemies of monarchy want to bring us through this concatenation of results, that hereditary

I

monarchy is an absurdity. What can I offer better in favour of aristocracy? I will not aſk you what Mr. Pitt has done, but what he has omitted, to degrade its true principle, to vilify the characters of its natural supporters, and in the persons whom he has admitted to a share of its privileges, (with very few exceptions,) to render it in the eyes of the people not only hateful, but ridiculous? again, when the House of Commons is held up to its conſtituents as an object of contempt, shall I hope to regain to it any portion of respect or attachment by repeating to them the language of Mr. Pitt? Or where, in his practice, shall I find arguments to contravert this detestable maxim, that the House of Commons deserves respect and veneration when acting with the Crown, execration and extinction when acting against it?

All this, Sir, is with me, the foundation of very serious alarms. I am concerned to see the constitution, which remember will be our best weapon of defence against France, in the hands of a man who will not give it its fair chance when opposed to brilliant and seductive, although fallacious schemes, cloathed in all the allurements of new theories, and imposing upon us with the authority of successful experiment. Much indeed has he to learn in the art of government, and much to unlearn of what has been taught him in the school of his youth, before he can attach men

to the constitution through him, and his mode
of administering it. When I hear in what
manner he describes it, and what he tells us
are its obligations, I am indeed alarmed for
the duration of its popularity, whether it be
offered to the choice of the people of England, or pressed upon their will. I certainly
am one, who, considering the circumstances
of the times, am ready to take the constitution *as it is*, and who, with the best wishes
for its wiser management, consider it not as
a thing to be tolerated, but as a thing to be
loved; yet when he tells me that it was the
constitution which made him minister in
1793, and that to keep him so, the constitution enjoins us to persist in those measures
which have marked the last three years of
our history with calamity abroad, and nearly
with the extinction of our liberties at home;
when I am told that to keep him in his place
the constitution demands of us to recognize
the debasement of the House of Commons,
and the proscription of all men who are not
ready to bow the knee to his usurped authority, then, I repeat, a fair chance is not given
to the constitution in any question which
may arise between it, and any possible speculation for its reform. What, in such a contest, are we tempted to hazard, we who
believe and know, that this is neither our
original charter, nor even so good a thing as
a clumsy copy of it? that it is something else

which ministers have fraudulently substituted
instead of a constitution, something which
operates not as a casual deviation from its
letter, but as a radical change in the substance
of the contract itself? I think this a great
evil: because in a struggle of such momentous import, reasons enough will be found
without furnishing a new one, for a cold
deadening neutrality, or at best a languid indifference to the event. Many there are
who, with an honest attachment to the constitution, will see nothing worth the trouble,
and still less the danger of a choice, between
the transient prevalence of projecting reformers, and the insolent dominion of a minister;—who will think that neither the one, nor
the other, have any claims upon them to stir
a step; but that they shall best perform their
duty to an establishment they love, and wish
to serve, by keeping their strength whole and
unbroken, until two mischievous factions,
exhausted by mutual animosities, shall present them with an easy victory over both.
Is this a thing to be wished? Would it not
rather be a symptom of ruin most rapidly
coming on indeed, if to any considerable extent a way of thinking were to prevail, which
should drive away well-intentioned men from
looking at all into the public affairs? Such,
however, must infallibly be the consequence
of separating whatever is distinct in public
principle, from a cause which is to pass under

the name of the constitution. Is it thus armed and accoutred, and under such auspices, that its real defenders can risque an engagement? And were it not the heighth of misconduct in those, who have so dear a charge in their immediate keeping, to venture with half their forces into the field, and link the fortunes of an odious and a powerless name with that of every valuable interest of their country? Can they think it quite safe to send about as a watch-word, the cry of PITT, OR A REVOLUTION?

Certainly it can never be with the effects of such a cry that I should recommend it to you to meet the dangers, whatever they are, to which we may be exposed by a French republic. God forbid we should not have some better standard than this to fly to when that fearful crisis shall come upon us! But the views of Mr. Pitt I must consider as the very reverse. No issue could be so favourable to him and his power. All his measures, therefore, will obviously be directed to bringing our public divisions to this point, and the nature of them will be such as may be best adapted to sustain the cheat of plots and conspiracies, and to feed the expiring embers of our fears. You will only be gainers by this in increased rigours of your government; the whole blame of which is visited upon your constitution, which it makes less dear to those who reason, and less worth defending to those who do not. It is hence that I have ever considered our former Whig associates to have fall.n into the worst of all possible mistakes when they coalesced with Mr. Pitt. For the first time since party has been known among us, and the name of Whig considered as the designation of that party whose way of interpreting the letter of the constitution was most conformable to its spirit, we hear it maintained, which that coalition does, as a principle of duty scarcely to be distinguished from their allegiance itself, that the crown having given its confidence to a particular servant, it does not become them to dispute his precedence. Thus in the preliminaries of their treaty with him they think fit to accede to a principle which vests in Mr. Pitt a perpetual title, and indefeasible right, to his office as a matter of property; to be governed by the rules and practice applicable to cases of property. Thus, shortly and conveniently are got rid of at once all that touches the merits, or that may hereafter affect the permanency, either of the minister, or the measures connected with him. That minister, and those measures incorporating thus with the machine of government, become a part of the constitution as necessary to it as the monarchy itself. To the holders of such maxims no middle course is left. They must take the whole of such a minister, or none of him: but in embarking with him at all,

A a

they must take the consequences of acting in
extremes. Then mark, Sir, what a sudden
and a frightful change is produced in the
entire complexion of your affairs! The
public voice is held in check by the imputa-
tion of seditious views to all opposition or
complaint. Even parliamentary dissent treads
close on the heels of disaffection. In this
temper it is easy to confound proceedings
which originate in mistrust of a minister,
with the incipient symptoms of revolt against
the sovereign. The alarm is spread at the
first movement which menaces that minister.
They fly to his defence as to the advanced
posts of the constitution itself. If the accidents of the times combine to invest them
with a decisive superiority in strength and
numbers, after repelling their opponents,
they become assailants in their turn. Ex-
pecting no quarter they determine to shew
none. Then is reared aloft the gloomy
standard of proscription and persecution.
The British constitution, disrobed of her
beneficence, and swathed up in *premunires*,
and confiscations, and constructive treasons,
is bid to display herself in the sullen majesty of terrors not her own. All choice between the extremities of evil is scornfully rejected from their plan of unconditional sub-
jugation. Rational neutrality becomes suspected. Timid hesitation is punished. The
feeble voice of moderation is drowned in the
din of a motley host of invaders, each yelling

out in his own barbarous accents, *he that is
not for me is against me.** They who set themselves to strive against this torrent, are accused, if not of positively participating in
the views of certain wild theorists, at least
of aiding and countenancing them in their
avowed designs against all lawful authority.
Who is prepared to submit to these pretensions ? Who will bear to be told that he cannot innocently seek a medium between the
claims of infatuated arrogance, and the menaced desolation of the change by which it is
proposed to resist them ? Yet it is by such
pretensions, enforced by such language and
principles, that those who on every consideration of talents, rank, character and property are the natural and stationary enemies
of projectors of all kinds, are disgusted and
driven to a distance. Men of warm passions,
listening to the suggestions of a just resent-
ment, throw themselves into the opposite
scale. An ardent popular spirit, nursed up
and encouraged by public distress, but hitherto without order or connection, by gaining
leaders and discipline gains all that it wanted
to effect the most extravagant of its purposes.
Parties and factions are formed, knowing as
little whence they come, as what they aim at.
Each, as it were, by instinct, finds itself em-
battled in hostile and opposite array. In this

---

* Vide the declaration of the Kings of Prussia and Hungary, delivered to the Diet at Ratisbon, May 17, 1792.

A a 2

universal soreness of the public mind CIVIL WAR is only deferred while a conscious inequality of force teaches prudence to the weaker side. But all is. prepared. They wait only until the folly of a minister, by swelling the mass of discontent, shall have increased their numbers to a capacity for action. Then, the first mistake in government is the signal.

I leave you to judge whether such is the ministry you would desire to see continued for its own sake? or whether you think it good for any purpose of maintaining the British constitution against reformers, French or English? Indeed the coalition which gave the Duke of Portland to Mr. Pitt, seems to have cut off for ever all hopes of this nature. Say what they will, the members of that coalition meet under impressions of such declared ill opinion, as totally to prevent their answering to you for the accomplishment of any one beneficial purpose by it. This is no common junction of parties the leaders of which consent to forget what might remain of animosity after the first cause of division had subsided. Mr. Windham in 1792—the interval is not too long for his consistency—told us that so far from thinking better of Mr. Pitt, one great motive for his supporting him was because he thought worse of him. Now what must have been Mr. Windham's opinion of the

sense of manly pride, of the political rectitude of a minister to whom in the face of
parliament he promises support and the oblivion of all contest about power or place,
lest a too great anxiety for the preservation of
them should distract his attention, relax his
energy, or keep him back from the adoption
of those strong but doubtful measures which
in the speaker's mind were so essential?
Doubtless Mr. Windham will acknowledge
that every thing which has happened since
that period, justifies the wisdom of that resolution, and confirms the minister's title to his
support. But are you prepared to follow up
all this strange reasoning to its consequences?
The ministry in 1792 was feeble, timid,
and improvident. To give it strength and
courage, he supported it. In 1794, it grew
worse. It shewed itself possessed of no capacity for the conduct, and actuated by no
right feeling towards the just object, of the
war. To make it better, and bolster it up
for a while, Mr. Windham and his friends
resolved upon becoming a part of that administration themselves. They hoped, it
seems, that although they should be compelled to sacrifice the whole principle on
which the Whigs had acted since 1784, they
might be able to make such terms with Mr.
Pitt as to secure them, though not pre-eminence in power, yet such a degree of strength
as would enable them to carry into effect

some of the leading measures of their system.
I would afk Mr. Windham with what fidelity
Mr. Pitt has executed those terms? and to
what degree he has enabled the division of the
Whigs who joined him to perform any one
of their engagements to the public, or in any
one instance, except perhaps in the admiralty
department, to better the system they found?
These gentlemen may deceive themselves,
but I assure you they deceive no one else,
if they imagine that their accession to office
has wrought any change in the character of
Mr. Pitt's administration. They have added
indeed something to its numbers : but the
great powers of government continue still
in the same hands. It is the same unnatural
faction that in the year 1784 joined with the
Crown, and that very mob it now threatens
to hang, draw, and quarter, to pull down
the House of Commons.

Desinat in piscem mulier formosa superne.

These may be very good reasons for Mr.
Windham to continue acting with it. He
and his friends may not despair of their efforts to serve you; but you, who are to
judge of the work, will probably expect,
both in shew and substance, something more
worth your money than a mere augmentation
of personal strength to the worst, and most
dangerous minister this country ever saw.

I remember the vast expectations which
you, and many other of my worthy friends
at **** had formed from that coalition. In
particular you thought what was to be done
for Ireland was of itself a sufficient justification of that step. Among other taunts it
was put to me, what must be thought of my
continuance in opposition to a government
which offered in their very names so many
securities for the public freedom? I agree
with you, Sir, that the objection demanded
some other answer than the general one,
with which however, so many of our rigid
examiners are satisfied, that my motives
were disinterested because opposition is not
the road to power or profit. In my opinion nothing can be more disgraceful than to
be seen continually in opposition to government, when it is good. I do not however
feel myself so very hard pressed for a reason
for keeping aloof from the Duke of Portland's union with Mr. Pitt last year. I
must think that whether it be regarded with
a view to principle or practice, the inefficacy
of any such union as was then proposed,
was plain from the beginning.

Unpropitious indeed were the auspices
under which it set out. It was but a sad
omen of success in their other projects that
forming this coalition, as they professed to
do, to preserve some very dear opinions,
they should have begun it by an act which

3

destroys the most valuable of them all. If they so much dreaded the prevalence of that insolent mob government which in common with every other distinction has pulled down that of character in France; could there have been a more fatal step than the ranging themselves under the banners of those whose lives have been spent in persuading the people that no such thing as character exifted? If the doctrine of equality, as practised in another country, was in truth so terrible to them, how can we account for their acceding to the political pre-eminence of a faction in this, who have so extensively corrupted the sentiments of our own public, and made them converts to doctrines derived from one common source with the purest, most genuine, unadulterated Jacobinism? What therefore, is it less than suicide in men, to defeat whose pretensions to power these heresies have been inculcated among the lower orders, to incorporate and identify themselves with the inventors of them, and under a weak hope of keeping at a distance principles which tend to equalize rank and property, give the sanction of their example to those which subvert from its foundation the only security they possess for rank, property, estimation, or comfort of any kind? I afk, what remains to them when the opinion of their public virtue is no more? I afk, in defiance of the flimsy conceits, and vain metaphysics on which Mr. Pitt's administration was erected, I demand, in the well-known accents of those who have left us to make a part of it, what laws, what establishments, what distinctions, nay even how long the liberal arts, or commerce itself can survive those perverted manners, and that vitiated state of society in which it is a received opinion that all men are alike,— that the service of our country corrupts our morals—that politicians and statesmen are all rogues, and the rest of those compendious maxims of calumny which form the basis and groundwork of the power of Mr. Pitt and his friends? To have been able to shew that in joining him they departed nothing from their own principle, they should have produced to the public a fair recantation, and a distinct, specific disavowal on the part of the minister, of all such notions. This act was necessary not by way of gratification to their own pride, but in order to discountenance those dangerous opinions which his elevation to office had rendered current. Instead of doing homage to him, the Whigs should have made him do penance to the constitution. I see no principle on which they could join Mr. Pitt before having exacted from him some sort of atonement, which circumstances perhaps might mitigate but could never supersede, except that which confounds all distinction of right

and wrong, and submits whatever we have
been used to look to as fixed upon the eternal maxims of justice, to the discretion of a
capricious and arbitrary convenience. You
afk me, whether I call this a desertion of
principle ? or whether it is any thing worse
than a mistake ? What can be worse than a
mistake on a subject so serious, I cannot
well imagine. If it will gratify any of them
to have it believed by one of their old friends
that they have not acted from sordid motives,
certainly I will not be the person to withhold the testimony of my sincere conviction
of it. What will be surmised by others who
have not the same opportunities of knowing
them, is not so clear. If the most uncha-
ritable opinions should prevail, they may
thank the industry of those to whom they
have united themselves. If the labours of
their whole lives should be resolved at last
into an unworthy struggle for power, let
them remember to whom it is owing that
this habit of thinking is become general
among the common people, and applied to
all men, and all parties alike.

But the mischief of this ill-starred union
does not stop here. It is not that it puts an
end to a party combined for certain objects
agreed among us all to have been highly beneficial, but that it discourages the hope of
forming any similar combinations in future.
It is not the public alone who will afk what

confidence can be placed in party professions?—Men who devote themselves to political life will afk what security there is in
party connexions? It is mighty well to answer that a truly independent mind will look
to no security from such quarters, but con-
fide in its own rectitude. All experience is
against these refined notions, and fanciful
modes of considering human actions as di-
vested of human motives. There are too
many discouraging impediments in the way
of those who resolve to fulfil their duties towards you, to admit of our lessening those
aids which are derived from the countenance
of illustrious names, and the general applause
of our fellow citizens. Much has been
written in favour of, and against, party connexions; and generally speaking, I have reason to think we differ very little in our opinions respecting them. Assuredly there is
no method which our conftitution tolerates,
of resisting with such good effect the daily
encroachments of aspiring power: because
the resistance of party is continued; whereas if you trust the cure of your public griev-
ances to the general operation of a spirit of
liberty, that cure will be uncertain, but your
risques without number. It will be always
a chance whether you can excite that spirit;
but a question deeply doubtful indeed, how
you can govern it. We must not conceal
however, that party connexions, by which it is

always best preserved and regulated, although
directed towards a popular service, never were
of an highly popular estimation. At court
they were in worse order still. A marked
proscription has very generally attended all
such engagements during the present reign.
Now figure to yourself, if you can, a situation more unpromising to those who mean
fairly your service, if, persecuted by the court
for steadily pursuing that service, and dis-
countenanced by the people under the impression that we mean only to serve ourselves,
ourselves should be the persons whom least
of all we can trust? Think what must be
the effect of rendering, as inevitably you will
when you destroy the principle of party
union, a feeble, intriguing, and distempered
court, the only market for the learning and
abilities of the kingdom? All but the mere
mechanism of politics will vanish from the
stage. No competition; no emulation; no
sense of glory; no fear of shame; nothing
to engage mankind to the state through the
medium of their virtues. No more shall we
distinguish in the mental attainments of those
who aspire, or are destined to eminent sta-
tions, that high cultivation so conspicuous in
the youth of our present day. The dull
stream of despotism will float down weeds
and rubbish to choak up every fountain of
intelligence. Literature will have no em-
ployment but an abject adulation of those,

who alone, and scantily, dole out the means
of its precarious existence. With every sense
of decent pride will perish all the energies of
manly genius. No little mischief will follow the total change in the object of our public animosities. Our contests, instead of
being continual but always confined to the
modes of administering a fixed constitution,
will be rare, but terrible, and every change
portend a revolution. Dark conspiracy will
succeed to open combination, and from the
principles of conspiracy, the gradation is but
too obvious to its weapons. Thus are the people separated from their legitimate guardians,
and delivered up to the artifices of every daring adventurer. In vain will it be hoped
that among so many opposite minds there
can be no union. When once these mistaken
men who have sought their own safety in the
destruction of their party have simplified
their differences with those they style the populace by reducing them all to one question,
and that a question between property and
numbers, the first projector that starts up
will give them all the union they need to
shew them their prey, and teach them how
to seize it.

I know there is a disposition to accede,
in the abstract, to most of these opinions.
But the times, it is said, call for unanimity,
and the oblivion of all former disputes in
order to save the state. Men who call upon

us for this in the loud tone of authority, think they have said enough when they declare this great work to be no party business. I am not so much surprised at hearing this language from the quarter from whence it comes, as at the sudden, easy simplicity with which it is adopted by those to whom it is addressed. Acting all my life in a party, and acting *with them*, I never understood, although I have often heard the sentiment pressed upon us by way of reproach, that when any one act particularly wise, just, or salutary was to be carried through, it became a matter with which party not only could have no concern, but which considerations of that nature would rather prejudice than advance. This is, allow me to say, a mere way of talking; a stale phrase picked out of that vocabulary of cant which we see now a days in the hands of every upstart pretender to public virtue. Party engagements are derived from no such sources of illiberality and bigotry. On the contrary; they are of a quality so opposite, as absolutely to exclude the influence of the nearest and the dearest ties unless associated with public principles. There have been times in our history when party was lost in the violence of civil convulsions. I do not think these have bettered your constitution. On the contrary : it always found great difficulty afterwards to recover its tone.

3

These, and other reflections upon the subject which the length my letter is grown
to obliges me to retrench, have long induced
me to consider party as a benefit and not as
an evil. It is good in its separation. It
is good, too, in its union with others;
when such union is proposed with a view
of preserving party in its objects, and
not of destroying those objects. Men who
engage with each other on these principles
are not at liberty to give up the public cause,
blended and made one with their private
honour, on any such hacknied invitations.
If at any time they should see a necessity
for assisting an administration they have
been used to oppose, they must beware of
taking a step which by destroying their own
characters will wholly preclude them from
bringing to government any accession of
useful strength. They must first be well
assured of that degree of change of system
which may leave them to the pursuit of
their own measures, without fear of in-
terruption. For this they must take securities in the name of the public, by pos-
sessing themselves of those official situations which, commanding an enlarged view
of the whole of our political situation, may in-
sure the means of carrying prompt succour to
its weaker parts. There are occasions, too,
on which they must insist upon examples. If
the minister whose measures they have
been resisting shall, with a view to his own

personal schemes, have raised and let loose against their party a wide, proscriptive, persecuting spirit, which operating possibly beyond his original design, threatens at length to subvert the whole fabric of our mixed government, he is not to be indulged in lamenting the difficulty of restraining it, or encouraged to call out to them for help without a fair recognition of his error, testified by descending from his post. This is no vain punctilio. It is to demand a sacrifice for the constitution. It is the point of honour, where honour is all.

Such were the only terms on which any union of the Whigs with Mr. Pitt could promise either safety to themselves, or eventual of stability to the government. They can scarcely be aware of the extent of what they have conceded. Instead of discovering any circumstances in these times which called for the oblivion of party animosities, they seemed to me to demand of us that we should preserve, with more than usual care, every trace and vestige of them. I thought it infinitely better to go on, as long as we could, with the old dispute of Whig and Tory, than teach men to refer all their causes of complaint to the distinctions of society, and to see only two classes in the state, and those the rich, and the poor. I know of nothing but party which can save, and treasure up the sentiments which help to keep these extreme disputes at a distance, nor can a true, party spirit, such as we have been used to recognize in this island, be extinguished, except through the operation of the most frightful changes. It is not that these changes can only be produced by public confusion. Dispositions to this effect may be silently and systematically encouraged among the people, teaching them indiscriminate mistrust in the professions of every man. When once their cast of thinking is thoroughly tainted with these suspicions, then is a revolution accomplished, without its tumults indeed but with all its consequences.

We used, my friend, to agree in better days, that the foundation for such a revolution was laid by Mr. Pitt in the year 1784. In my conscience I think that we owe, to the example of that calamitous period, every mischief the country has suffered from the debility of its government at the beginning of these troubles, and from its intemperance now. Then began in effect, and was avowed with all the insolence of power, that system of proscription and monopoly through which a corrupt court draws to its own use the whole authority of the state, which it divides and parcels out by a rule of favouritism to the exclusion of all claim from birth, merit, or services of any kind. To keep this engrossing spirit alive, the worst of

C c

all factions was nourished among the most
infatuated of all people. The House of
Commons, not in its construction but in
its institution, was treated with still less
ceremony than ever it has been since in the
speculations of the most fanciful reformers. The constituent body was encouraged to look for direct aid from the
crown in all disputes with its representative.
These thoughtless politicians reserved no
provision for cases in which they should
have to maintain their own ground against a
faction they were stirring up to destroy the
influence of the middle ranks. What has
followed was natural. The fair, Whig aristocracy is nearly reduced; the court and
the mob have quarrelled; and it is now next
to a question whether the whole of your
government shall not be demolished. To
this issue at least they are bringing the contest, unless means be found to stop them in
the course of their insane guilt.

You have here, Sir, the reasons of a very
plain man, a friend to practical politics, for
adhering with what has been esteemed a criminal pertinacity to the principles in which
he was educated: who pretends to know
little of their abstract value; but having
always found that they led him to consistency in your service, feels that he has no
other wish than that they should continue to
govern his conduct. What would be a re-

medy for the evils of which he thinks your situation full, is more than he has the presumption to pronounce. He is far from confident that all remedies will not come too late. One opinion he is not afraid to risque at all events, and that is, that no very great good is to be expected from an unlimited and implicit confidence in the king's ministers. Whether any better issue may be looked for from a change of men and measures, is a point on which he is by no means unreasonably sanguine. Such an event alone, and supposing it not to arise from a conviction of past errors on the part of both crown and people, he is satisfied would produce only a short suspension of calamity. But the people have much to atone for towards others, before they can be true even to themselves. Suddenly to demand the services of men against whom they have sucked in with malicious relish every species of calumny for these last ten years, to receive that service with ungracious hesitation, to dwell upon its benefits with cold applause, and then probably, in conjunction with a treacherous court and a fawning faction, to turn short round upon us with some cry of fancied mischief, and consign us to disgrace and banishment for the rest of our lives, this, let me tell you, is neither in the right of any people to require, nor, I sincerely hope, in the folly of any men who value their reputation to comply with. They who are in earnest must come fairly forward with the symbols of penitence as well as conciliation. They who now discover the mischief of tearing asunder the legitimate ties which bound them to the constitution, must resume them with fresh endearments, renovated by a sense of their former folly and misconduct. With gratitude in their hearts, and an honest welcome in their looks, they must turn towards the man whom no threats, no temptation, no injury, no galling memory of ill-requited service, whom not the sacred voice of friendship itself has for one moment biassed from the steady line of his public duty. But unless they resolve to co-operate with him effectually, all effort will be vain: without retarding the fate of our country it will only enhance its severity, and sharpen the appetite of our enemies with the desire of revenge as well as dominion.

If I could see a prospect of their doing this, I should not so entirely despair of the commonwealth. But while there exists a disposition either in the court, or among the people, to temporise with the vanity of a minister, and to pass by all other services lest the delicacy of his ambition should suffer the pain of some humiliation, then is there a ruinous infatuation, and far-gone depravity indeed in our general habit, against which all

3

further conflict is useless. Who will answer for the consequences? These can be
measured by the times alone. With no me-
diatorial party to modify the pretensions of
an irritated and ill-governed people against a
weak and misguided court, if those to whom
we look for support fail us at this crisis of
their fate and our's, if they go on trusting
these men until the wide questions of popular rights gain the ascendancy, who will undertake that the multitude shall distinguish
the mischief from its cause, or settle, in the
balance of their inflamed passions, the blame
due to the faults of their government, and
that which belongs to the administrators of
it? This, whenever it comes, will be the
worst of all dangers. We shall not even
come to a question upon our constitution.
It will slip from under our hands: leaving
us to lament the ignominy of so losing it,
with the aggravated misfortune of discovering that we shall not have avoided the horrors
of civil strife.

: It is your business to look to this. For
me, whatever may be our common destiny,
I shall be numbered with those who have
done their utmost to avert this, and every
other calamity which has already befallen
you. I shall reflect with comfort on having
seen to their end the public obligations I had
contracted with you. With no hand in the
rash measures which precipitated the fall of

(198)

the Whig party, I have followed it to the grave in sorrow and mortification. In attending its obsequies I have borne, it is my firm opinion, my share in the last mournful rites of the constitution itself. Death can push his victory no further. Farewel, Sir! After all, I think we have meant the same thing; and that if the present situation of our country left any room for hope, we should not differ in devoutly wishing for an administration which could give us an honourable peace, upon safe terms, which could defend us against France after peace, and provide, both in precept and practice, for the perpetuity, as far as it is in human wisdom, of the free government of this country in all its branches.

F I N I S.

E R R A T A.

P. 5. l. 4. for *even* read *ever*.
9. l. 12. for *suppress* read *surpass*.
12. l. 29. for *mischevious* read *mischievous.*
59. l. 8. for *this debate* read *the debate*.
do. l. 18. for *meditate* read *mediate.*
70. l. 11. for *in* read *to*.
71. l. 24. for *as the degree* read *as to the degree.*

BOOKS printed for J. DEBRETT.

A COLLECTION OF STATE PAPERS RELATIVE TO THE WAR AGAINST FRANCE now carrying on by GREAT BRITAIN, and the several other EUROPEAN POWERS; containing Authentic Copies of

Treaties,	Remonstrances,
Conventions,	Official Letters,
Proclamations,	Parliamentary Papers,
Manifestoes,	London Gazette Accounts
Declarations,	of the War, &c. &c. &c.
Memorials,	

In Two large Volumes. Price One Guinea in Boards.

⁎ In this Work is inserted many important STATE PAPERS which are not to be found in any similar Publication. This Work will be continued with the same Degree of Accuracy and Care during the Continuance of the War.

Octavo EDITION of EARL MACARTNEY's EMBASSY, This Day is Published, the Second Edition, elegantly printed in One Volume 8vo. Price 7s. in Boards,

A NARRATIVE of the BRITISH EMBASSY to CHINA, in the Years 1792, 1793, and 1794; containing a faithful, interesting, and impartial Relation of the various Circumstances of the EMBASSY, with an Account of the CUSTOMS, and MANNERS of the CHINESE; and a Description of the COUNTRY, TOWNS, CITIES, &c. &c.

By ÆNEAS ANDERSON,

Then in the Service of his Excellency Earl Macartney, K. B. Ambassador from the King of GREAT BRITAIN to the Emperor of CHINA.

" We have travelled with Mr. Anderson through the whole of his Volume with great satisfaction, and we do not hesitate to recommend the same pleasure to others. He may, perhaps, by some be thought too minute in his descriptions; but in an unknown country, which China may in a great degree be considered, every circumstance is important; and in such a Work as this, where there will necessarily be an occasional dearth of great objects, or at least where such objects want that bold variety which can be communicated to the page, trifles become interesting, and aid the general effect of the narration."
EUROPEAN MAGAZINE, May 1795.

LETTER from the Right Hon. CHARLES JAMES FOX to the WORTHY and INDEPENDENT ELECTORS of the City and Liberty of WESTMINSTER. 14th Edition. Price 1s.

A JOURNEY in the Year 1793, through Flanders, Brabant, and Germany, to Switzerland. By C. Este. 8vo. Price 6s. in boards.

" We recommend this Journey to the perusal of every one who wishes to acquire a perspicuous and competent knowledge of the Countries that have so frequently called up the attention of Europe, and were never more than at present the Objects of general regard." EUROPEAN MAG. Jan. 1795.

REPORTS of the COMMISSIONERS appointed to inquire into the FEES, GRATUITIES, PERQUISITES, and EMOLUMENTS, which are or have been lately received in the PUBLIC OFFICES. Price 7s. in boards.

The HISTORY of the ORIGIN, PROGRESS, and TERMINATION of the AMERICAN WAR. By CHARLES STEDMAN, Esq. who served under Sir W. Howe, Sir H. Clinton, and Marquis Cornwallis. In 2 vols. quarto, illustrated with 15 plans, &c. Price Two Guineas in boards.

Number XVII. of the DEBATES of the LAST SESSION, revised and collated with the Notes of several Members, the PARLIAMENTARY REGISTER; or, the History of the Proceedings and Debates of LORDS and COMMONS; containing an Account of the most interesting Speeches and Motions, authentic Copies of all important Letters and Papers laid before either House during the LAST SESSION.

The

Books printed for J. DEBRETT.

The PARLIAMENTARY REGISTER of the FIRST, SECOND, THIRD, and FOURTH SESSIONS of the PRESENT PARLIAMENT, from 1790 to 1794, in twelve volumes, octavo, Price 5l. 14s. 6d. half bound and lettered.

The PARLIAMENTARY REGISTER, from the General Election in 1780, to the Dissolution of Parliament in 1784, in fourteen volumes. Price 5l. 5s. half bound and lettered.

The PARLIAMENTARY REGISTER, from the General Election in 1784, to the Dissolution of Parliament in 1790, in thirteen volumes. Price 6l. 12s. half bound and lettered.

The DEBATES and PROCEEDINGS of BOTH HOUSES of PARLIAMENT, from the year 1743, to the year 1774. Printed uniformly to bind with the Parliamentary Register. In seven large volumes, 8vo. Price 2l. 12s. 6d. half bound and lettered.

MILITARY REFLECTIONS on the ATTACK and DEFENCE of the CITY of LONDON; proved by the Author to have been the most vulnerable part of Consequence in the whole Island, in the Situation it was left in the Year 1794. By Lieut. Col. GEORGE HANGER. Price 3s.

REPORTS of ALEXANDER HAMILTON, Esq. Secretary of the Treasury, read in the House of Representatives of the United States, January 19, 1795.——Containing a Plan for the further Support of Public Credit, and for the Improvement and better Management of the Revenues of the United States. To which is annexed, The Copy of an Act for making Provision for the Support of Public Credit, and the Redemption of the Debt. Printed by Order of the House of Representatives. Price 4s.

SPEECH of Mr. SMITH, S. C. on the Reduction of the Public Debt, December, 1794. Price 1s.

Mr. SMITH's ADDRESS, in justification of his conduct. Price 1s.

AMERICAN KALENDAR for 1795. Price 2s. 6d. sewed.

The FEDERAL CONSTITUTION of the UNITED STATES, with an Appendix. Price 2s. 6d.

AMERICAN PHILOSOPHICAL TRANSACTIONS, 3 vols. 4to. Price 2l. 17s. in boards.

The FIRST and SECOND LETTERS from EARL FITZWILLIAM to the EARL of CARLISLE, fully Explanatory of his Conduct in Ireland on a late important and memorable Event. Price 1s. each.

Mr. FOX's SPEECH in the House of Commons on the State of the Nation, March 24, 1795. Second Edition. Price 1s.

A QUERY whether Certain Political Conjectures and Reflections of Dr. DAVENANT, in 1699, be, or be not, applicable to the present Crisis. Price 1s. 6d.

The WORKS of JOHN HALL STEVENSON, Esq. containing Crazy Tales, Fables for Grown Gentlemen, Lyric Epistles, Pastoral Cordial, Pastoral Puke, Macarony Fables, Lyric Consolations, Moral Tales, Monkish Epitaphs, Essay on the King's Friends, &c. &c. including several Poems, now first printed from the Original MSS. with Notes, and a Preface by the Editor; illustrated with a View of Crazy Castle, and the Constellation, engraved by Milton; elegantly printed in Three Volumes, small octavo. Price 15s. in Boards.

A FULL REPORT of all the PROCEEDINGS on the TRIAL of the Rev. W. JACKSON, at the Bar of his Majesty's Court of King's Bench, in Ireland, on an Indictment for High Treason; containing the Speeches at length of the Attorney General, Messrs. Ponsonby and Curran, with the Documents and Letters at full length given in Evidence; and also the Inquisition and Verdict, with a Copy of a Paper found in the Pocket of the Prisoner after his decease. Price 3s.

9082   6

www.ingramcontent.com/pod-product-compliance
Lightning Source LLC
Chambersburg PA
CBHW030831270326
41928CB00007B/994